SELECTED
MEMORIES

READERS COMMENTS

This collection of essays/stories is a treasury of thoughtful observation, at once wry and uncannily wise. Our author's curiosity, plainspoken prose and tantalizing snapshots, allow us to accompany him on amazingly diverse geographical and cultural adventures!
— JUDITH MARGOLIS
Artist / Essayist;
Creative Director, Bright Idea Books

I have known Jim Breivis for 50 years, first as a parent in my small school in San Francisco's Haight-Ashbury, and since then as a friend. I always have seen him as someone with a good memory for telling tales of years gone by, and as a person with a great sense of humor. Both qualities shine through in this memoir. His book takes the reader through numerous adventures that most of us only can imagine. I read through it all quickly as if it was an adventure of my own.
— STEVE ZOLNO
Author and Retired Healthcare Administrator

Readers will shiver in awe at Jim Breivis's adventures. The author's stories and color photos of people and places are so dramatic that readers will wonder whether such wildly different cultures will ever blend. Others will believe that, if humanity is to survive, those diverse cultures had better find a way to get along.. Most of us spend our lives doing deep career dives. Jim Breivis did that, and more. An orthopedic surgeon by profession, Jim spread his wings wide enough to see the world in his time off, large chunks of time he took without looking back. With Diane, his wife, Jim forged another life away from medicine, to which he always returned.. Fly with Jim and Diane as they hear a well sing in Kenya, read Jim's toast to Diane in Bukhara on her birthday, help them track elusive tigers in India, and witness a piercing religious ceremony in Malaysia.. Jim didn't have to range through jungles to witness the bizarre. It was next door in San Francisco. Sit with Juror-Jim at the murder trial of "Susie Q" in San Francisco's superior court.and you may never leave home again.   — LOU SALOME

Friend, Classmate, Newspaperman,
and Author

SELECTED MEMORIES

A COLLECTION OF TALES & ADVENTURES
FROM TRAVELS AROUND THE WORLD

By James Breivis

REGENT PRESS
Berkeley, California

[paperback]
ISBN: 13: 978-1-58790-695-4
ISBN 10: 1-58790-695-3

[e-book]
ISBN 13: 978-1-58790-698-5
ISBN 10: 1-58790-698-8

Library of Congress Control Number: 2024950751

Cover Design by Timm Sinclair

Manufactured in the U.S.A.
REGENT PRESS
Berkeley, California
www.regentpress.net

CONTENTS

PART TWO
Non-Travel Related Memories

For Diane

My Lifetime Partner and

Travel Companion

INTRODUCTION

I n this collection of stories and articles written over a thirty-four-year period the subject matter has varied, with no connection amongst them as to topic or theme. Prior to elaborating on them, though, allow me to first tell you a bit about myself.

In the mid-1930s my parents settled in Binghamton, New York. They had met in Rochester, New York while my dad was in medical school and my mother in nursing school. Thirty-five years later this pattern was repeated when I married nurse Diane while I was in Albany Medical School. My father had grown up in Binghamton; he readily established himself as a primary care physician and the county coroner.

It is possible that my interest in travel writing was subconsciously influenced by my dad. It was years after his early death at age 47 (when I was 11 years old) that I discovered his self-published book about his mid-1920s travel to visit his family roots in Lithuania. Of great interest and admiration for me is that he was able to pay for this trip by working as a butcher on the passenger ship S.S. *Lutzow* which took him from New York to Bremerhaven, Germany.

Without interruption, after I graduated in 1958 from high school in Binghamton, New York the next fourteen years were devoted to my education and training to become an Orthopedic Surgeon.

I, and then subsequently we, resided in Worcester, Mass., Albany, N.Y., Milwaukee, Wis., Rochester, Minn., Spokane, Wash., and finally San Francisco.

As mentioned earlier, I met Diane while in medical school. For supplemental income there I worked as an I.V. technician in the Albany Medical Center Hospital. One afternoon I received a request from a nurse (Diane) who needed an I.V. started for one of her elderly patients. Soon after we were dating. In those days when I donated blood to the blood bank, I would receive $25. We would go out to dinner with that largesse.

We were married a week after I graduated and now, 58 years later, we continue to share adventures as we enjoy our senior years. Our four children – Adam, Sarah, Molly and Aniwa – are wonderful human beings with intellectual curiosity, kindness and compassion. They, along with our granddaughter Kaleigh and son-in-law Adam Paul, have joined us on many trips to far-away places. A wonderful experience in learning and sharing.

Until I retired from the San Francisco Kaiser Permanente Medical Group in 1999 I practiced general Orthopedics and also served as Chief of the Department, Assistant Chief of Staff of the Medical Center and was very involved in local, national and even international medically-related organizations and efforts.

Diane and I had always looked forward to travelling together, and before my retirement had thought we'd done a lot. The so-called big-time trips started in 1999 when she sold her business (wedding and event planner). For the next twenty-five years and still counting we have either rented out our San Francisco home for months at a time, or, for the past ten years, done home exchanges.

The adventures included living for weeks to months in London, Marrakesh, Prague, and Bali.

It was Samuel Beckett who wrote, "Words are the clothes thoughts wear." So appropriate a lead into my introduction to writing.

I have never had any formal education in writing skills. This may become evident when you start reading my stories. The majority of them are travel-related and there are two points that I want to emphasize. The first is that none of the stories were planned before any particular trip. It was only after such-and-such happened that I decided to document it.

The second point came to my attention only after writing for a few years. Because Diane and I had the time and resources to travel independently (by necessity we did do some group travel), stories such as "Sweet Potato," "Hluhluwe" and "A Taste of India" could never have been documented via a group experience. Such accounts, by their nature, come from very personal encounters.

The predominantly independent travel mentioned above came about by way of circumstances and luck. It started with the Kaiser Permanente Medical Group's letter in 1999 of an enticing early retirement offer to senior physicians. Within three months I retired, Diane sold her event planning business, and we left home for months at a time (once for 18 months). And by renting out our home while experiencing other countries and cultures, the renters were paying our way!

Destinations varied often by whim. For months we rented in London, Marrakesh, Prague, Bali and too many other places to count. Visits to India became a favorite. We even flew around the world by taking advantage of an airline partner program that allowed stops practically anywhere.

Once I decided to write about a particular person or experience I did just that. Advice written by the great Irish playwright Brendan Behan at the Dublin Irish Literary Museum hit home with me. Essentially, his recommendation was to just keep writing down your thoughts and fine tune it later.

While assembling my stories for this book I realized that there are so many topics I could have added. For instance, doing volunteer surgery on an infected hand in the West African country of The Gambia I was charged for the instruments and medications. Attending a costume ball in a castle in southern Poland was like a scene from a movie. Attending a weeklong cremation ceremony in Bali was very special. The list is long.

There are two very dramatic stories that I have purposely never recorded. Just too personal and painful. One involved my sustaining a perforated bowel while flying over the Atlantic. I knew it when it happened and yet was more or less trapped. This situation is often lethal. The other incident happened while Diane and I were on the Mexican island of Isla Mujeres. We went swimming in front of our hotel sometimes and decided one afternoon to have a pre-dinner dip. The beach was empty and there were no boats or fishermen. The undertow literally swept us out to sea. The shore progressively got smaller and our fatigue greater.

I vividly remember expressing our love for one another and saying good-bye.

My memory of the sequel is spotty. Perhaps it was an adrenaline rush like one reads about. I remember repeatedly grasping Diane and flinging her toward shore over and over. Her being alive probably urged me to continue. And she was relatively limp, which was probably a blessing.

The next thing I remember is both of us lying at the water's edge experiencing breathing, each other, and relief. We were alive.

Documentation of memorable trips or particular events are reminders of a period in the past when you saw or experienced something special. I hope you enjoy these souvenirs.

Part One

Travel Related Memories

SWEET POTATO

❖

From 1975 to 1979 between 1.5 and two million people, approximately a quarter of Cambodia's population, were executed or died from starvation under Pol Pot and his Khmer Rouge regime. This gruesome personal story was obtained as a result of our wish to do some bird watching.

Sweet Potatoes

He stole the sweet potato because his family was starving.

We met Cheong Try (he said "call me Tree") because he was recommended by our hotel owner in Kampot, Cambodia. We had asked at the hotel bar for a guide for some bird watching. Eric, the hotel owner, recommended Try with the comment, "A very nice and interesting guy."

Try's family knew the risk but shared the sweet potato anyway. Three hours later Try's father, mother and sister were murdered.

Kampot, which is in southern Cambodia, is what I call a "close to" town. Close to more popular places such as Kep and Sihaunokville and also close to the old French Hill Station on Bokor Hill. But the mountain road up there had been closed for a month. And, as for the world-famous fields that produce pepper, well, that's in Kampot Province.

Kampot is just a sleepy town that most tourists ignore. Lonely Planet states, "Kampot's most enjoyable activity is strolling along streets that evoke days long gone." After the hustle and bustle of Hong Kong and Phnom Penh, this place in March 2009 was a welcome change.

Kampot is close to the Gulf of Thailand. Officially it is on the shore of Prek Kampong Bay. Nowadays the waters have been overfished and the locals have turned to harvesting salt from the fields of salt water that lay exposed to the blister-

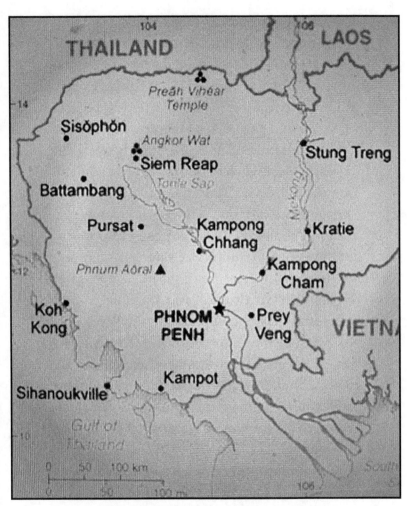

Map of Cambodia (Courtesy Cambodia Tourism)

ing heat. It was in these salt fields early the next morning that Try pointed out some birds.

Words such as gentle, polite, assured and

content come to mind when I think of my impressions of Try. Like so many Cambodians, he looks young. At first I thought he was around thirty years of age. I was off by over twenty years. Around five feet five inches, maybe 120 pounds when wet and always in a long-sleeved shirt and long pants, tattered but clean. And when he talks to you, he looks directly into your eyes, and you soon learn that you want to hear it all.

It turned out that Try did not know the names of the birds. We didn't care. Oh, we indeed saw some beautiful bee-eaters that day and two trees full of rare nesting Sarus cranes. But the highlight of that day was listening to him and seeing Cambodia through his eyes. He was living in the community and from him we learned about the government versus private schools, Buddhist festivals including weddings and feasts, the crops, family traditions and much more. He often started a sentence by saying, "In my country …".

Cambodia does not have a patent on horrible war stories. It's a pretty awful history, however, especially over the past fifty years. Try's personal story was the authentic version of what the rest of us can only imagine.

Between 1969 and 1973 Cambodia was incessantly carpet bombed. All by the U.S., and officially Cambodia was not a declared enemy of the U.S. This, plus civil wars and a whole lot of confusing, unfortunate circumstances led to the country being controlled by the Khmer Rouge. The latter tortured and killed thousands of their own countrymen: first the wealthy and intellectuals, then the politicians and middle class, and thereafter anyone who had aligned themselves with the hated Americans.

Try's family were peasants, and that group was uprooted and sent to slave camps. Objections or any hint of disobedience meant death. Food was plentiful but none of it was for the peasant slaves. The crops were for export and to support the army. Peasants such as Try were fed meager rations; many starved to death. Such was the situation in 1977 when Try stole the sweet potato.

I had to watch as the soldiers tied up my mother and father, covered their eyes, and then killed them with blows to the back of their heads. My sister and I were then tied together at the wrists, blindfolded and pushed along a path.

"Two young soldiers soon untied the link between us. I pulled off my blindfold and decided to run toward the nearby forest. With every step I expected a bullet to hit me. I do now know why they did not shoot."

(I suspect they had plans to rape Try's sister

before killing her.)

On that day in Kampot, Try spoke to us in a matter-of-fact manner. We met two other Cambodians later that month with similar gruesome personal accounts and the delivery demeanor was similar.

"Later that night, I returned to the village. My sister was also killed. I knew that I had to hide. The forest was my only choice."

Try then told us how the days became weeks and then months. He slept during the day, often in trees, and moved every night. If he heard voices in the forest he did not dare respond because even fellow peasants might turn him in. Any peasant who hid or protected anyone was immediately killed. Food was not a problem because of wild fruit and plants.

After about a year, he heard different sounds outside the forest. The Vietnamese Army had arrived and repatriated Cambodia. The Khmer Rouge had fled westward, close to Thailand.

"They cleaned me up, cut my hair and fed me. They made me join the Vietnamese army. I wanted to flee but the Vietnamese shot deserters, and to identify me as a Cambodian in their army I received a totoo on my chest."

Try showed us his rectangular tattoo, near his collarbone.

Photo of Try

"I fought in their army for four years. In 1981 I left their army and worked for the U.N. deactivating landmines.I was very good at it. Only one accident."

Try showed us the many scars on his left leg from surgical repairs by a German volunteer surgical team. He was lucky. Cambodia is replete with amputees. As of 2008, the average number of land mine injuries remains around 750 per years.

Try now has four children and works as a trekking guide around Kampot. He smiles a lot and is so happy to have a wife and four children. When we parted, he thanked us for visiting Cambodia and hoped we would someday again visit "his country."

JUST A LITTLE OFF

❖

I t grows and you cut it. Could be lawns or hedges, but in this instance, I am talking about hair.

Prior to most trips away from home one obtains a haircut. When on the road for months at a time, the ritual of choosing a stylist (a.k.a. bar-

Author getting a haircut in Chile

ber) followed by the experience can transform a rather mundane task into an adventure. Most of this story took place in Budapest.

The attention that the flock of epithelium up there garners has always intrigued me. Look at any newsstand rack of magazines and hair "coverage" (a pun, I guess) rates up there with exposed breasts.

Over the years I have been inclined to find a particular person to perform the shearing and have reliably returned to them with a sense of comfort and satisfaction. Influencing factors in this decision have included post reduction positive comments, interpersonal experience, accessibility, and just plain vibes.

Well, a lot of the criteria used to select a barber – oops – a hair stylist (that correction alone allows a 50% markup) had to be thrown out the window on our 18+-month trip around the globe in 2000-2001.

So far, in no particular order, my hair has been "refashioned" in Krakow, Hanoi, Budapest, Marrakesh, Istanbul, Mexico City, London, Chile and back home in San Francisco.

Selecting a suitable site, establishment and person for the event can be a time-consuming and difficult task. Oh, sure, that stuff up there will always grow out. True, but there are extremes.

For the most part each episode has been un-eventful. The 80-minute job in Marrakesh where I received two shampoos and meticulous attention to the beard, nose and ears along with mint tea was noteworthy because Diane was rushed through in 20 minutes. But after all, she was a woman in a Muslim country. And speaking of my ears, in Istanbul the incessantly smoking, tea-drinking barber not only threaded away each stray hair in each ear – by then, I was willing to confess to any accusation – but he also conclud-ed by finishing my ear canals off by passing his maximally lit Bic lighter in and out repeatedly.

Hair salon in Budapest
(Courtesy photo from Budapest Salon Hajas Hair.)

My experience in Budapest was particularly memorable. Diane and I had by now chosen to make concomitant or successive appointments for our scalp revisions. This in itself was unique, after doing it separately for over 35 years. We had decided on Budapest over Prague after reading how upscale Budapest had become post-Russian domination.

We actually made appointments at two candidate Budapest sites. The "winner" was selected after we staked out each place and made note of the neighborhoods, customer flow and how the existing customers looked. (We have subsequently become less obsessive.)

Diane went first while I sipped mineral water and glanced at magazines – yep, showing all the fashionable and fanciful hair styles.

When my turn came the young lady gave me an ever-so-brief smile and asked me something in Hungarian. At least I think it was Hungarian.

What I wanted was just a trim and I said so, but of course to her I could have been commenting on the weather or the latest news event. So, while arranging myself in the chair, I put out my right hand and with my thumb and index finger demonstrated the small amount of length to be removed.

She said something highly suggestive of "OK"

and I relaxed with the hair style magazine as she went about her business.

It was a only a few minutes into the procedure that my attention was torn away from that suspenseful magazine. I think it was the sound from above similar to a Toro lawnmower that did it.

The bottom line was that the length of hair REMAINING was the same dimension as I had earlier demonstrated BETWEEN MY THUMB AND FOREFINGER.

THE SYRIAN EMBASSY IN TEHRAN

❖

The official at the Syrian Embassy in Tehran listened as I presented our situation and request. I mentioned our experience and the advice given to us a month earlier when we visited the Syrian visa office in Damascus. I emphasized our very positive impression of Syria and its people while visiting as tourists just prior to coming to Tehran. I suggested that he must have the power to expedite the issuing of our re-entry visas to Syria. He said he was awaiting a response from Damascus and could not act on our behalf without permission from his superiors.

At this point I must say that I was skeptical regarding the truthfulness of his response. To be blunter, I was sure he was lying. Of course, I did not express this thought while sitting in that office of the Syrian Embassy in Tehran.

The encounter mentioned above requires delineation. Here was our saga.

In 2010 my wife Diane and I made a multi-month trip that included Lebanon, Syria, Iran, and Jordan. As it turned out, we had to add another destination that was never intended. In fact, we had to look up exactly where that destination was on the map.

For U.S. tourists to visit Iran an Iranian-approved tour company must handle the procurement of visas and submit to the Iranian government a detailed itinerary with the understanding that a licensed guide would accompany us the entire way.

Fair enough.

Syria had no internal travel restrictions for visitors at that time. However, if you wanted to leave the country for a short amount of time and then return, the traveler needed to obtain an additional "re-entry" visa. This is a key point in our story.

Many have asked, "Why would you ever want to go there? Aren't you concerned about your safety?" In 2010 the answer was "no." That area of the world was the cradle of civilization. It is replete with unique and wonderful remnants of history including religious, archeological, tribal, and other cultural treasures. Our expectations and optimism were rewarded tenfold. We felt safe throughout our travels.

The scheduling gods dictated that our desired time in Syria would be interrupted by our tour of Iran. Our itinerary therefore had us flying to Tehran from Damascus via Syrian Air and then returning to Syria upon the completion of our three-week visit in Iran. The only requirement was the re-entry visas.

A few days before our scheduled Tehran flight we hired a local to take us to the Syrian visa office in Damascus to obtain the re-entry visas. After hours of queuing in various departments we were told that since we already had standard visas that it would be best if we simply stopped at the Syrian Embassy when in Tehran and that they would quickly supply us with the necessary paperwork. This turned out to be BAD ADVICE.

So, the day after arriving in Tehran, our Farsi-speaking guide took us to the Syrian Embassy. It is located on an incline on a busy boulevard, and access for us was only through an opaque sliding window protected by bars. This communication opening was about seven feet above the ground, so not only were we always looking up to try and converse, but the official serving the public often closed that window for no apparent reason and left the people waiting for it to reopen. Very annoying.

Eventually we were told to fill out some applications and submit 87,000 Syrian pounds (approximately $200 each). The official said that the forms would be sent to Damascus for approval, where we had been just a few days earlier, and that we could pick them up in two weeks. Since we were about to tour Iran for three weeks, we felt confident that the Syrian return visas would be processed and ready for us when we returned to Tehran.

Our travels around Iran were wonderful and uneventful. The people were extremely congenial and hospitable. The image of Iran presented in the western press did not coincide with our experience. So very true, also, with Syria.

Prior to our scheduled flight back from Tehran to Damascus we had four days to experience Tehran. The pre-arranged agenda included many cultural stops and other points of interest. Most of it never happened.

For two consecutive days we were craning our necks outside of the Syrian Embassy, hoping for access to the bureaucrat behind that opaque window. Sometimes we waited an hour. The eventual response was always, "No word yet from Damascus. Perhaps tomorrow."

We were in a bind. In a few days our Iranian visas were going to expire. We could only imagine what our plight would be if we remained in that country with expired visas. Our guide shared our concern. We simply had to get beyond that barred window and plead our case. Within that fortress someone in charge had the power and authority to issue our two return visas to Syria.

Perhaps at some risk, our guide demanded that we be allowed to speak to the Syrian official in charge. To our surprise we were eventually ushered into a thickly carpeted office. My wife Diane, our guide and some embassy folks were purposely seated in the back.

Behind an ornate desk was an official projecting an image of authority. Also, boredom. Behind him was a huge picture of Bashar al-Assad, who I swear was looking down at us and smiling. Perhaps laughing.

As stated in the beginning, I was sure that the embassy official's statement that they needed to hear back from Damascus in order to assist us was "baloney." Nevertheless, our session was over. As we filed out of that room, he looked me in the eye and said, "I hope you still feel positive toward Syria and its people."

Our guide and driver plus Diane and I sat dejected and silent in our car outside of the

Bashar al-Asad

Syrian Embassy. Based on the Iranian visa stamp in our passports, we had two more days in Iran. Any attempt to obtain an Iranian visa extension would be futile because it was the Islamic New Year, and all government offices would soon be closed. Syria was no longer an option.

We eventually decided to visit the offices of Syrian Airlines. On the way we drove past the former U.S. Embassy with its various forms of "America is evil" murals. Photos were forbidden but I snapped away anyway.

The Syrian Air offices were in a large building. Uniformed employees were in a pre-holiday mood as closing time was imminent. Our guide found a woman employee who spoke some English and listened to our story. We inquired about flights out of Tehran within the next two days to any country that did not require a visa.

No luck. She did find a flight in three days with two seats. We were desperate. Perhaps both the Iranian and Syrian immigration agents wouldn't pay much attention to the dates showing on the visas in our passports. We thought it was worth a try.

"Book us, please." Realizing our plight, she waived any charges but did insist that we visit the Syrian Air visa offices before any tickets were issued. We were ushered upstairs to these offices.

Painted exterior wall of former U.S. Embassy in Tehran

Our guide explained our situation to two and then three officials who studied our passports. They were impassive and we were nervous.

I will always remember the scene in that office. A manager and his assistants kept looking at our passports while concomitantly holding a wall calendar. And they were counting off repeatedly with their fingers. Two, three, even four times. They said something to our guide and walked out. The outcome of all this was a mystery.

Our guide only indicated that we had to

hurry back to the ticketing area.

Back down in the airline office our tickets were printed, handed to us, and we were wished a Happy New Year!

In the car our guide told us that it so happens that the first day of a stay in Iran, at least from a visa standpoint, is not the day of arrival but the next full day. This meant that when we passed through immigration at the Tehran airport in three days our visas would not have expired. So what if we could not return to Syria (and a suitcase we had left behind).

Government building with flag, Baku, Azerbaijan

As our Syrian Air flight left the tarmac Diane and I smiled and put our heads back on the seat rest. Baku, the capital of Azerbaijan, was a very interesting place. Getting there was half the fun.

BLACK FRIDAY

❖

British Guyana (now Guyana) lies on the north-
ern shore of South America, just east of Venezuela.
In 1965, I spent the summer there along with four
other medical students via a program arranged with
the U.S. Government (A.I.D.). This story is about
a wooden sculpture by a Guyanese artist depicting
the then recent riots and bloodshed during elections.

ritten by the Sculptor:

> "*The general contour of the work is in*
> *the shape of a left side boot symbolizing*
> *that the people's understanding was on*
> *the left, which is always the side repre-*
> *senting evil.*
>
> *The eye with the red cup represents the*
> *Peoples Political Party which was in*
> *power at the time of the great controversy.*
> *The other eye represents the sun, the sym-*
> *bol of the limited force, which was the*
> *chief factor of opposition at that time.*

The stripes on the nose represent the pointers of a broom which was the symbol of the P.N.C., Peoples National Congress, that played between the two parties in the 1961 general elections.

The nose there is the symbol of inspiration, you may see that the various symbols travel from the eyes through the nostrils to the higher regions of thinking which are symbolized by three cloudy eyes, showing how the sympathetic and merciful powers of the people were blinded at the time by their diverse political ideas.

The long red stripes coming from the eyes represent the sorrowful tears of those that lost their properties in the terrible fires.

The things like stockings under the cruel mouth symbolize that it was real Christmas for those that looted the stores while it was death, sorrows, tears and imprisonment to others."

Black Friday

Selected Memories

I came across Black Friday in Georgetown, British Guyana (now Guyana) at the artist's studio in 1965. I was a medical student serving a surgical fellowship at the Georgetown Hospital. I was immediately attracted by both the sculptor and this carving and purchased it immediately. Because of the complexity and details of the art, he agreed to write out his interpretation for me and glue it to the back of the piece. Now, 59 years later, I have copied the script because I see that time has yellowed his original copy.

Not only did this represent the first piece of art that I ever purchased, but it was also to be a gift for my then-girlfriend and subsequent wife Diane (it will be 58 years this year).

There is another story concerning Black Friday. It involves the Professor of Surgery from NYC who came to British Guyana as my instructor soon after I acquired the carving. He loved and wanted it so much that he asked me daily to sell it to him. Although somewhat intimidated because of "rank," I refused. After three or four weeks he approached me and said that if I sold him Black Friday that he would give me an "A" for a grade.

I still have Black Friday and did not get an "A."

NAKCHUNG
AND THE BEAR

❖

This account took place in Bhutan, a landlocked Buddhist country wedged between India and Tibet. In 2012 I was a volunteer Orthopedic Surgeon at their national hospital in the capital, Thimpu.

He scurried to the nearest tree and climbed it as fast as he could. But he was not fast enough. There was a heavy blow to his left foot, and then searing pain. Almost like peeling a banana, the bear had pulled skin, tendons and some bone in a downward motion and Nakchung fell to the ground.

He reached for his foot but before he could get to it the bear was tearing at his scalp.

Nakchung, the 34-year-old cattle herder from the very remote Bhutanese district of Dagana, pushed and screamed and the Himalayan black bear released its grip.

It was on my third day of orthopedic rounds at the Jigme Dorji Wangchuk National Referral Hospital in Thimphu, Bhutan that I chose Nakchung to interview. I thought that any one of the other twenty to thirty patients would also qualify, but the bear mauling was too inviting. It was my hope that an interview might give me more insight into this unique land and its people.

Bhutan, with its 740,000 people, is wedged in between India and Tibet. Dzongkha, the native language, uses the same script as Tibetan but is sufficiently different that Tibetans cannot understand it. English is spoken by the educated because it is taught in the schools.

I am indebted to Tshewang, one of our Orthopedic Assistants, for his willingness to be our translator.

When I asked Nakchung what happened when he shoved the bear, a smile suddenly appeared. "He ran away." He acknowledged that he did not know why, but that for sure this was a stroke of luck. He recollects lying on the forest ground for quite a long time, bleeding, hurting, and not thinking too much about what to do next.

It was about an hour or so later, with nobody in sight, with the forest silent and with the blood from his scalp giving his mouth a salty taste, that he remembered his cell phone. He reached for it, found it, and dialed his brother. He was in an area with no coverage.

There are a few national highways in Bhutan. That's the good news. Landslides, large potholes, blind switchbacks, and huge trucks to and from India and Bangladesh make 30 mph seem like a wish that will never come true. In Nakchung's home district of Dagana there is no need for a road map because there is only one paved road. To my question, "How far from your home to any road?" he replied, "About four hours."

He knew that he had to move and get help. He managed to stand for a short while and then fell to the ground because of the pain. His flip-flop shoe was full of blood and his scalp was hanging near his left ear. He crawled for a while but navigating over fallen logs, formidable stones, and up and down inclines made for slow progress. There was no choice. At least the sun was warm, and he could see. Minutes turned into hours. Somehow, he got across a river and kept his phone dry but lay exhausted on its bank. Now flies were buzzing around his head and ankle. He wanted to sleep. He tried again to reach his brother and this time his brother answered. After describing his location, he slept on that riverbank for the next two and a half hours.

At a Buddhist Temple in Bhutan

Health care in Bhutan is improving. For instance, from 1985 to 1990 the infant mortality rate dropped from 103 per 100,000 to 55. In the same time frame life expectancy has risen from 43 to 66 years. Yet even today (2012), with a population of 750,000, Bhutan has only one cardiologist, one neurosurgeon, and few trained emergency physicians. About 65% of Bhutan is forest. The rural areas have only minimally educated personnel handling "anything and everything." One wonderful piece of health-related information is that in the past year the Thimphu referral hospital has not seen any patients with gunshot wounds. Zero.

When his brother and a friend arrived at the river area, they found Nakchung moaning and barely able to walk. Their destination was the only health care facility in the district. After two and a half hours of carrying him across two rivers, up slopes, down slopes, and with a few rests, they were not at the medical clinic but had reached their home. After a short rest, minimum nourishment, and some dry clothes they did more of the same, namely up and down through the forest, crossing one more river two times, and then three hours later they arrived at the clinic, which was staffed by a medical assistant.

The bear had ripped about 60% of

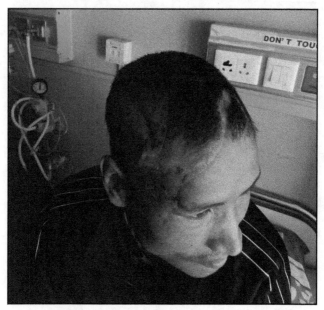

Nakchung in hospital with healing scalp

Nakchung's scalp into a flap with its attachment near his left ear. The medical assistant, with minimal training and maximum common sense, gave her utmost attention to the scalp. Washing, cleansing, removing grass and debris and tacking down the flap was done over the next two days. Meanwhile, she saw that his left foot was missing a lot of skin, some bone and also tendons. She called Thimphu, the capital, and requested an ambulance. One was dispatched immediately and three days later Nakchung became the last patient in row B on our Orthopedic Ward.

As I write this Nakchung's scalp looks like one would expect, but it is healed. His foot needs some reconstructive orthopedic and plastic surgery attention, all performed by Orthopedics, but he should someday be back in his forest area tending to his dairy cows.

In the morning on hospital rounds he smiled at me and told Tshewang that he was happy that I listened. So am I.

— October 2012, Thimphu, Bhutan

A frequent sight in Bhutan

THAT SOUND

From London to western Europe by train under the English Channel. This trip provided the stimulus for this travel story with an unexpected event.

Trains have always had a particular fancy in my heart and mind. I vividly recall stretching out the car window in our family car as a child to wave at the engineer of a passing freight train. And if the man in the caboose (now that is a great word that is heading for extinction) waved back, it made my day.

There was also my Lionel train set in the basement with its engine that sent out smoke (with the help of smoke pills) and the coal car, the lumber car, and the oil tanker.

For the most part, trains are no longer a major mode of transportation in the U.S.

As I reflect on the many train journeys that Diane and I have taken during our wanderlust years I can come up with a long list of adventures. There are many candidates for the most memorable. Before I comment on that choice, I would like to mention some of the top candidates for outstanding experiences.

The overnight overbooked Oslo to Bergen, Norway trip for which we had no tickets, no reservations, no local currency and of course, no seats.

The Mumbai to Aurangabad scene where amidst the strewn bodies, the squalor, and the sight and smell of human waste within the Mumbai railway station, we sighted a beautiful white-breasted kingfisher sitting on the wire above us.

And there is always the adventure of purchasing tickets. Too often this represents the

Train waiting to depart

highest mountain to climb in a foreign country. For instance, while waiting in line or "queueing" for our Warszawa to Zamosc (Poland) tickets I eventually learned that the only way one moves up in line is by standing to the extreme right wall adjacent to the ticket window. No exceptions.

The train story that I have chosen to highlight, somewhat paradoxically, is our June 2000 London to Brussels Eurostar trip.

The departure area at Waterloo station with its restaurants, its crisp, polished, and uniformed attendants, escalators and ample directional signs allowed us to glide right into our assigned car.

We were soon properly situated in our roomy and comfortable seats in the car directly behind the locomotive. This location would turn out to be significant.

This mode of travel between London, Paris, or Brussels is very rapid and obviously relaxing. A perfect opportunity to get through the Times and the Observer or Independent, if not more.

At this point in the story, I must ask the reader if they have felt sounds? By that I mean have a visceral "feel" associated with a sound. I have, we did, and that is why this train story stands out amongst many others.

As I indicated, the Eurostar moves fast. Real fast. The daylight coming through our train windows told us that we had progressed beneath the English Channel and were zipping through northern France.

Diane and I had just traded newspapers when there was a most unusual sound. And again. Then three or four more times, very rapidly. I "perked" my ears and listened intently, somewhat analogous to a deer or rabbit lifting their head from their tasks. But now there was silence.

I thought we had repeatedly struck a tree branch. Diane thought it was the train wheels crunching gravel.

Now the train suddenly stopped. We waited. The conductor announced that there would be a temporary delay. Outside the train window police began to appear and walk around somewhat aimlessly.

Even to this day, and I am certain forever, I will FEEL that sound. They go together. Because that sound represented the noise from a horrible suicide.

THAIPUSAM

The following events took place in 2006 just outside Kuala Lumpur, Malaysia. Diane and I were visiting a friend who was a member of the Malaysian Ministry of Health. He and I had been board members of an international organization dealing with health technology assessment and we were following up on his gracious invitation to visit his country.

Our host and his wife are devout Hindus, in a predominantly Muslim country. We were honored to accompany them to the very holy Hindu temples located upon a mountain where they worshipped, and we observed the holy festival of Thaipusam.

During Thaipusam Hindi devotees seek blessings, fulfill vows, and offer thanks in honor of Lord Subramaniam, who represents virtue, youth and power and who is the destroyer of evil. Some undergo incredible rituals in pursuit of their beliefs.

The following is my account of what we saw at the festival of Thaipusam.

Initially I had not noticed the assembled crowd near me because I was concentrating on a very spiritual site previously described to me as the mountain, which housed a Hindu temple. Throngs of worshippers, laden with offerings, were climbing the 272 stairs leading to their destination, which was housed within the mountain's Batu Caves.

Meanwhile, near us at ground level, the soaring midday temperature of Malaysia made a few observers seek some shade, but most maintained

**Golden statue of Tamil Hindi Lord Murugan
in front of the 272 stairs to Batu Caves**

their position in the open near the chanting men. The steady beating of drums was not random but purposeful.

Diane and I were fortunate to position ourselves near the front to see the spectacle that was capturing the attention of the gathering throng. Just as we arrived, we observed a man pass a sharp metal skewer through the flesh of the man standing in the center. That spear or skewer went into his flesh just above his posterior pelvis near the kidney and exited just to the side of his spine. A similar one had been placed earlier over the other kidney.

Other attendants or assistants were working diligently to place hooks into each of the man's arms, especially below the elbow and shoulder. And there I was, ever so close, snapping pictures and moving around in a circular manner to see the progressive placement of the approximately 18-to-24-inch skewers into the flesh of his chest, abdomen, back and neck. The man was wearing only a dhoti. Over and over, I watched his eyes, his forehead, his fingers. He remained passive. As the tip of each spear and the end of each hook entered his skin and progressed into more flesh, he never changed his appearance.

It was one of acceptance. The beating of the drums was accompanied by chanting. The Malaysian sun was relentless. Soon the metal skewers were attached to an external frame or cage called a kavadi, and high above his head a crown of multiple peacock feathers was added.

I thought of my experience in orthopedics with external fixation frames applied with sterile wires through bone to stabilize pelvic, spinal or long bone fractures.

We always used anesthesia!

Researchers in other settings have found that the temperature in the feet of those who walk on

Devotee in trance receiving burden

Another view of burden

hot coals is actually lower than normal. There is no scientific explanation. Common to that spectacle and the man described here is a trance-like state.

Diane and I counted over one hundred skewers and probably as many hooks that entered his body. Those placed through his tongue and cheeks made me shiver. None of the piercings resulted in bloodshed. His attendants periodically pulled on them to make sure the "hooked flesh" was in tension. His trance-like state was remarkable.

The devotee firmly believes that by undergoing this ritual he will wholly be under the protection of the deity, who will not allow him to shed blood or suffer pain. The piercing of the tongue renounces the gift of speech so that he

Devotee about to climb the 272 stairs

may concentrate fully upon the deity.

The final segment for the kavadi carrier was a climb up the 272 stairs to the Batu Caves. His chanting attendants protected him during his ascent. Heavy pots of milk had been attached to each side of his frame and would be left within the caves as an offering to the deity.

A BIRTHDAY
SALUTE

Uzbekistan is in the center of the Eurasian continent and is known for its mosques, mausoleums and other sites linked to the Silk Road. This caravan route was the primary trade route between China and the west from the 2nd century B.C. to the 15th. The Uzbeks are very devout Sunni Muslims. When we visited in 2005 they were forced to speak Russian instead of their native tongue.

Following is my birthday toast given to Diane on April 10, 2006, in Bukhara, Uzbekistan at our travel group dinner. Russian was the predominant language, so I gave it a try — well, sort of. 90% of the Uzbeks are Muslim. As the level of vodka in the bottles progressively lowered, and the clapping receded, I stood and delivered my creation.

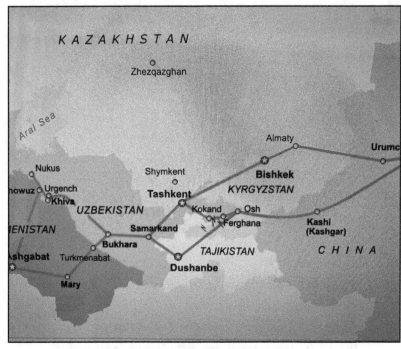

Map of Uzbekistan and the Silk Road
(Courtesy of National Geographic Silk Road Travel Tours)

Uzbekistan roadside scene

Diane and Jim in Bukhara

Sweeping the grounds

The radish lady at the market

Beauty is in the eye of the beholder

James Breivis

No one would have thought
Way back in '43
That this year it would be celebrated
Amongst the proud Uzbeki

Sixty-three seems risky
To those with fewer years
Tonight, let's say "Shest 'Desyat Tri"
It just sounds better in "Russky"

Age is nothing more than attitude
Glasnost is recommended
Let's drink to that "openness"
And pour forth the platitudes

Tho from many places we are from
It is here in Bukhara
That we raise our glasses to you Diane
And say, "Assalamu Alaikum"

VEINTE KILOS
Y MAS

❖

It was the type of scale one usually sees in a small fish market. We all watched as the young man hooked the bananas to it. As he struggled to lift the heavy load, the arrow moved left to right and then sort of settled in one place, and he said, "veinte kilos." Twenty kilos. That's forty-four pounds. He then moved along the dirt path, lifted more bananas, made some adjustments with a swing of his machete to get to another veinte kilos, and eventually nine identical piles of plátanos (bananas), held with rope to a yoke, awaited their fate.

It is close to noon and the sun here on Rapa Nui (Easter Island) shows little mercy. Earlier, a two-minute shower and its cooling effect proved to be just a tropical tease.

It is celebration time here on the island and we are in a particularly special location to observe the first of two events that has the small sun-screened crowd camera ready.

It is February and each year two weeks are devoted to honoring the traditions and culture of the Rapa Nui people. Called the Tapati Festival, it consists of many dances, music, body painting, strength and beauty competitions that are highly exciting as well as well attended.

Easter Island belongs to Chile, but its social order and ideology are all Polynesian – fittingly so, since this is Polynesia's easternmost point. This has been well demonstrated during Tapati because the delightful Polynesian influence is everywhere. Night after night we listened to the music of Oceania and watched the dancers sway their hips and undulate their arms and torsos to the rapid beat. At times it is hypnotic.

The special location for today's Tapati competition is Rano Raraku. We climbed the rim of a volcano and descended to the reed-filled lake that fills the dormant crater. A few hundred yards behind us, sentinels of the past lay strewn along the outside wall of the volcano. They are the megalithic 30-to-80-ton Moai, the stone statues that provide more questions than answers to their history and placement. Many books with theories are available about the over 800 Moai on Rapa Nui. Here at the quarry of Rano Raraku, which is part of the volcano wall, the many Moai cede their stardom for a few hours to the event we are about to watch.

Like the stone in this area, the nine young men who are about to participate in the Tapati triathlon are solid. And they are totally naked except for small palm leaves or cloth patches.

**Moai on Easter Island —
erected between 1400 and 1650 A.D.**

**Contestant with veinte kilos of Bananas
— Easter Island**

With their bronzed skin covering perfect muscle masses, their jet-black hair neatly tied, and with handmade reed canoes slung over their shoulders, they look like their ancestors must have appeared.

From the far end of the lake the first triathlon segment begins with each of them seated upon their reed canoes. They come toward us by stroking with ancient paddles, disembark upon reaching the shore, and then begin their first run around the rim of the volcano. No Nike shoes here. Barefoot and with the veinte kilos (44 lbs.)

of bananas now slung across their shoulders, each man progresses onwards. As I watch these descendants of past warriors handle the sun, the path, the weight, and their competition, I experience all sorts of emotions and feelings. I feel their aching shoulders, backs and thighs.

After the long lap and just in front of us each hero drops his load of plátanos (bananas) with a thud. This brings a look of temporary relief to them that immediately switches to determination as the final phase of the triathlon begins.

For about a half mile they sprint to the upper rim of the volcano. We can see how fatigue negatively influences speed. The spacing between contestants increases.

After rushing up the path and about a third of the way around the lake, each runner then picks up a pre-positioned bundle of tied reeds and continues with it down the path to the far end of the lake. There, the long bundle is placed in the water and the contestant lies prone on it. The end of the race is now in sight with "only" the lake to traverse. This final segment is not a swim because they cannot use their legs. Alternating arm strokes – left, right, left, right – there's maybe 20 minutes of this agonizing repetition.

For the seventh consecutive year the winner has been the same young man. With a string of flowers placed around his neck he postpones more accolades until he can greet the other men as they finish. Such is the spirit of Tapati.

After the many photographs and hugs, each fatigued participant heads home. Along with pride and satisfaction he also may keep as many bananas as he wishes (and can carry).

Later that afternoon we moved to Maunga Pui, which is a steep grass-covered volcanic hill and the site for the Amo Maika competition. It is from this hill that natives clad similarly as in

Contestants crossing the volcanic lake

the morning will construct their own banana-leaf sleds and zip, bump and fly down while on their backs, holding onto the sides of the sleds for dear life. We watch from the bottom and cheer and clap with each successful run. This time the event is recorded by crews from Japan and France.

After the Amo Maika competition we had about two hours to prepare for the evening festival of music that ended around midnight. And so went that day on Rapa Nui at the Tapati Festival.

DIAMOND IN
THE ROUGH

Romania is barely mentioned in high school history texts. Western press coverage has been minimal. I vaguely recall the accounts of the Ottoman Turks depicted as the bad guys, Dracula in Transylvania, the Hapsburgs and of course, the uninvited Russians. Later, with the assistance of the Soviets, the Romanians then got Nicolae Ceausescu. Eventually he and his wife were executed in 1989 after more than two decades of repressive rule. Throughout history Transylvania, a large part of what is now central Romania, has been like a semi-inflated political soccer ball – alternately batted about or left along a curb and ignored.

The ancient Romans, Hungarians, Saxons, Turks, Russians, and of course the Romanians have all laid claim. The Carpathian Mountains have served as both a barrier and a destination.

In World War II Romania was a major source of oil for Nazi Germany and was heavily bombed by the Allies. Yet, after the war, Truman and Churchill chose to not fight for its freedom from Russia because allegedly Romania was just not that important to them.

In so many ways, Romania continues to be in a sorry state. As on a beaten wife or abused child, the scars run deep, and many are permanent. They exist physically and in the psyche. Hundreds of years of damage is difficult to conceal or overcome.

During our visit to this enigmatic country in 2006 we saw former political prisons, roadside memorials to loved ones who had suddenly disappeared, and destroyed neighborhoods. In Bucharest we visited the "People's Palace" built by the megalomaniac Nicolae Ceausescu while Romanians were dying of starvation.

Despite such damage and the lack of modern amenities, Romania provided us with wonderful sights and encounters. Our daily experiences stimulated us to read and read and ask and ask.

I miss carts and horses. In this agrarian country they predominate and even have the right of way on all Romanian roads. The crude wooden wagons are typically about twelve feet long and in them one sees stones, logs, earth, or hay. Usually "Papa" sits in front while "Mama" rides with her legs dangling over the side or back. Both are dressed like their 1915 predecessors, or maybe even 1875. One wonders if they have clocks or calendars back in their humble homes. What for?

And then there are those horses. Every day we observed them slowly but consistently fulfilling their mission, pulling loads sometimes so heavy that the driver walked alongside. To dampen the sound of passing cars the farmers place bright red mop-like tassels just behind each ear of the horse.

One day I noticed something strange as I passed such a wagon. No driver anywhere! I slowed down, pulled over, and watched as the wagon methodically approached, passed us, and turned left off the main road. Only at the last moment did I see the owner lying asleep in the body of the cart. No matter. The horse knew where home was.

On another occasion I decided to stop and give an apple to each of two horses that stood at the side of a country road. They crunched those red babies for a while, dropped them, and then looked bewildered. My suspicion is that apples are saved for the people and the horses felt guilty!

If the many storks in Romania could talk from their nests, they would likely say the auto drivers below are all drunk. What they typically see are cars constantly zigging and zagging, swaying, thumping and crawling. None of them stay in any lanes. What on earth is going on?

Common scene in Romania

The answer is easy. The decrepit roads are so full of giant pits and holes that drivers constantly swerve to preserve their tires, rims, and other auto body parts. And at any moment a driver (me, for instance) could suddenly encounter a flock of sheep blocking the entire two-lane road.

May 1 is "May Day" and is still a national holiday despite the departure of the Russians. On a long walk that day in the country village of Enisala we had two wonderful "people experiences." It was our good fortune to have with us a Romanian native who also spoke English.

The first encounter surprised us because a woman came rushing out of her old wooden home as we passed and presented us with a bouquet of beautiful flowers from her front garden. This woman was just happy that we were there. Alex, our translator, told us to notice that the total flower count was always an odd number unless one was placing flowers at a gravesite.

"Baba" in Romania with welcome offer of home-made wine

A few minutes later on that same road we met three "Babas." After being in Romania for a while we appreciated how much the Babas contributed to the visual picture of the land. These older village women were returning from the cemetery where one customarily leaves wine and a specially made cake at the graves of loved ones. These ladies talked and talked, showed interest in who we were, and insisted on giving us some of their leftover home-made cake called coliva and wine. The coliva contained wheat, sesame seeds, almonds, ground walnuts, cinnamon, sugar, pomegranate seeds, raisins, anise and parsley. And the wine? A courtesy sip was more than enough! More important was their sincere welcome to us at their village and home site.

Evidence of Romania's long history is everywhere. Near Brasov, huge 14th-century Saxon churches and monasteries are well worth visiting. The thick walls around these sturdy structures were constructed for protection from the invading Turks.

East of Transylvania is Bucovina and its world heritage painted churches. Most are in rural areas and are cared for and managed by nuns. Like pearls within shells, the churches lie within encircling walls. Painted on the exteriors of the churches are stunning frescoes of

Bucovina monastery (16th century)
religious frescoes with religious motifs

Countryside dance rehearsal NW Romania

complex themes with glorious colors. Some are
in their original 15th-century state. Historians
say that these frescoes at Voronet (thus the origin
of voronet blue) and Sucevita were placed there

for the non-Christian soldiers to learn about Christianity before being sent out to fight the invading Turks. Every time I saw such a pearl I felt awe and appreciation. What beauty! How did they build and create them? How have they survived so many threats over the centuries? How lucky I am to be here.

Tucked into the northwest corner of Romania is Maramures. Nowhere else in the world have I observed wood so respected, loved, crafted and preserved. From the roadside one can observe houses built as sturdy domes with interlocked beams that have survived centuries of harsh winters. And like special cakes, the basic structures are beautifully decorated with intricate hand-carved wooden lattice on the porches and windows with their own special, unique and fascinating adornments. Separating these homes from the road are immense carved wooden gates that illustrated the social status and wealth of the inhabitants. Years ago, the royal landowners erected them to protect the safe interiors of their homes from the evils outside. Closer inspection reveals carvings such as the tree of life, birds, and even snakes. Some homeowners still place money, incense, holy water and religious statues around these structures.

On a beautiful spring Sunday morning we

travelled the country roads of Mara Valley in Maramures to villages with names such as Surdesti, Plopis and Budesti. We sought out the ancient, tall-steepled Greek Orthodox churches that are nestled adjacent to dirt roads, with chickens scurrying around, and few cars. All overflowed with worshippers. We sat with them, observed, shared the moments and appreciated the scenes.

In so many ways Romania is hard to describe. Its history, its turmoils, its struggle to simply survive. But then there is the beauty. Truly, a diamond in the rough.

Common fence and doorway in Maramures in NW Romania

A TASTE
OF INDIA

❖

In the far northern part of India, close to the Himalayan origins of the Ganges, is Shimla. Because of its cooler mountain climate, it served for many decades as the summer capital of India. One morning Diane and I decided to take a walk towards a nearby Hindu temple.

Davender Garg was also heading to the Jakhu Temple. We met him as we were walking up the paved mountain road high in the hills of Shimla. The forests around us consisted mostly of tall pine trees, and if one were guessing with only photos, they could easily say we were in northern California around Lake Tahoe.

Our progress was somewhat slow because at 6500 feet we had yet to be acclimated. Our new walking mate slowed his determined and direct pace to chat with us and explain the intricacies of Hanuman.

Davender Gard, our companion to the Jakhu Temple

More than 700 million people practice Hinduism and 80% of the people of India are adherents. It really defies any easy definition, particularly to a mind nurtured in Western traditions. Hinduism has no founder, central authority or hierarchy. To be a Hindu you must be born one, so there is no proselytizing.

As we ascended higher and higher on the switchback course Davender described his daily morning prayers with his parents in their Shimla home. There, the family had a shrine devoted to Shiva, one of the facets of Brahman.

Today was special because in his hand he was carrying a bag that held a plastic container that originally was intended for water.

Now it served as a receptacle for the mixture of cow urine, feces, butter and cream which soon would be blessed by the temple priest at Jakhu. After this morning's blessing he and his family would use it every day during their prayer sessions.

Cows and white bulls roam freely in India and have been worshiped since ancient times because they represent fertility and nurturing, and thus benign aspects of the mother goddess and a symbol of Mother India.

There are over 300 million deities in the Hindu pantheon, so no belief or worship gets neglected. Each has an object of veneration often chosen by the largest or key benefactor of any particular temple. Since Hindus believe in rebirth (called samsara) and the quality of the rebirth depends on one's karma, they believe that some Hindus can or will return in an animal form. Perhaps a bat or a rat or a monkey.

Shimla is a northern city with a cool climate that formerly was the summer location of the Indian government. It allowed the legislators to carry on their functions away from the heat in Delhi. It also was a former British Hill Station.

Our destination, the Jakhu Temple, is devoted to the monkey god Hanuman. We wanted to visit it because of its importance to so many of the Hindu people of India. Meeting Davender allowed us to obtain a lot of detailed information about what we were about to witness. He was so very honored to inform us, and we were appreciative to receive.

After about twenty more minutes of walking and talking we began to see the buildings connected with the temple, as well as all the monkeys. They were in the trees, on the road, and running about. Suddenly one of them was on Davender's shoulder snatching his spectacles. This all happened very fast, but Davender knew what to do; so did the monkey. Up the roadway a bit the monkey handed back the eyewear in

Monkeys at the Jakhu Temple

exchange for a bag of candy mixed with rice that is sold to worshipers to use as an offering when they enter the temple.

The monkeys were there as, well, sort of invited and honored guests. After all, any one of them might be a reincarnated former ancestor or friend. In other temple visits we had observed such protection of and deep respect for bats and even rats.

The final climb was steep, and the pathway moderately crowded with devotees. We could hear the distinctive clang of the temple bell and smell the aroma of incense.

The appearance of the temple surprised me. It had a plain exterior and was the size of perhaps a standard Starbucks. At its base a broken wooden door with only one hinge revealed the area where we were to leave our shoes. At least it offered some protection from the inquisitive monkeys.

Navigating the stairs to the metal temple door was a bit arduous because we had to dart and dodge monkey waste while clutching our day packs. At any moment I feared being the victim of a monkey snatching.

The floor plan of the structure was essentially a box within a box. An altar with statues, flowers and multiple lights, including a blinking neon model, occupied the middle of the building. Sitting astride the inside doorway to this altar area was the temple priest. He was listening intently to a young man and woman, presumably a married couple, as they related some form of concern to him. Behind the priest was a painted portable telephone with a crank like the ones seen in WWII war movies.

There were about eight others in the temple along with Diane and me. Davender prayed in front of the various wall paintings that depicted some form of monkey-to-man-to-monkey transformations and then he knelt in front of the priest. He waited patiently for the couple to finish their deliberations and when this indeed happened, he gratefully allowed the priest to take the bovine contents into the room with the altar for the blessing.

We sat on the carpeted floor and just observed. I still had to clutch my day pack because monkeys were scurrying around amongst us.

Somehow through all of this the atmosphere was one of solemnity, and despite our only being observers, we felt paradoxically participatory.

Davender's container, which was at the feet of the priest, was now opened. The priest placed its contents on the forehead, closed eyes and the lips of both Davender and the aforementioned couple. Davender then moved back to where we were and asked if we wanted to share in this ritual.

Diane and I politely refused, hoping that nobody would be offended.

Later, as we descended the mountain, Davender happily answered our multiple questions about what we had witnessed. He told us that we were the first Americans he had ever met. I was not sure how to interpret that. He seemed to be thrilled to have interested outsiders inquire about Hinduism and this particular deity.

At the bottom of the hill we exchanged names and acknowledged the pleasure of each other's company. I took his photograph but left out the plastic bag and its contents. The picture in my mind will suffice.

A FIRM
BUT RISKY
DECISION

❖

Within twenty-four hours after landing in Florence in the spring of 2023, the number of family members joining us was scheduled to become seven. This travel-related story describes our sudden dilemma of not having an affordable place to stay.

T he Santa Croce pedestrian walkway had to be navigated carefully because of the weaving of bicycles, the gelato-eating locals trying to decide if the next lick should be on the top or on the periphery, and a few children kicking soccer balls.

It was only three hours since the three of us disembarked from our flight. With Kevin, our Airbnb rep, we navigated the well-worn stone steps to the prearranged four-bedroom suite that would be our lodging for over three weeks.

It took four attempts to successfully handle the door lock and enter. It then took about thirty minutes for us to declare "No Way." No blankets; chairs absent on the first floor; no bed covers; no art on the walls. No Wi-Fi, no bedside stands, and overall, it was full of "No's."

Kevin seemed to understand. His offer to obtain blankets and Wi-Fi was not sufficient. Our investment was at risk, we understood, but daughter Molly, Diane and I were united in our decision. But what next? In the next 24 hours four more family members were due to land in Florence.

Jet lag and such a shocking disappointment are not a good combination. The situation called for one or more remedies, and quick ones.

In a few days our dear friend Paul was coming from Milan to have a visit with us and had booked a room at the Hotel Casa Botticelli. Without a clear alternative we went there via taxi and secured three rooms for Lord only knew how long and at what cost. At least it was a start.

The Hotel Casa Botticelli had been the home of a descendant of the artist and owner of a large antique gallery. It boasted extraordinary paintings throughout, with fine sculpture and objects

James Breivis

A walkway in Florence

placed with precision and taste. All of the rooms had modern plumbing and the touch of class. We had total comfort with luxurious atmosphere for $125 per night per room. In-season that rate went up to $250.

With the most immediate crisis solved, we had to sleep despite our hunger. Obviously we still had a lot of tasks ahead of us, but the mind fog had to be modified.

In such situations the location of the minute and hour hands on your wrist does not really

Florence with its Duomo

matter. In so many ways consciousness is determined by some external force. It was in the middle of the night (I guess) that I was awakened by Diane either exorcising or exercising her tablet. "I think I found us a new apartment."

Awe, amazement and doubt occupied the consciousness previously mentioned. With the original contract formally declined, a formal description and appeal process in place with Mastercard, and some amazing determination and vigor, Diane headed out at 0900 with just-arrived Adam Paul (our son-in-law) to inspect the prospective new four-bedroom rental site at Via San Donobi 55.

I am writing this fifty-four hours after our Flight 2656 touched the tarmac. With her near-fluent Italian Diane charmed the elderly alternative apartment owner and by that second evening the seven of us were very comfortable as we munched on Italian sweets in our huge new comfortable dining room.

A few months later we received a full refund for the payment to the first landlord. We were able to show Mastercard that what had been advertised initially in writing was simply not true.

HASSAN WAS FROM ALEPPO

❖

Traveling alone (just Diane and I) so often makes solid new friendships develop easier. This story about our meeting Hassan is an example. It was 2010; a few months later a devastating civil war broke out that destroyed much of Aleppo, Syria. Hassan and his family lost all their possessions and barely made it out of the country.

We left San Francisco for the Middle East in January 2010 with measurements in hand for a new hallway carpet. It was our intention to purchase a new runner in either Syria or Iran.

Eventually we were at the fringes of the Aleppo, Syria souk (which, by the way, is one of the oldest such shopping areas in the world) when Hassan (full name omitted for his safety)

Hassan with Diane in Aleppo

walked towards us. He and a colleague were looking for customers. By a happy coincidence for him, we were heading to his store anyway because of a prior recommendation.

Hassan, with his fluency in English and Italian (along with Arabic and other languages) impressed us with his intelligence, interests, courtesy and general demeanor. He certainly was different than most with his Italian and Syrian/Jewish heritage. And his smile would melt an iceberg.

His shop was small, with eclectic choices ranging from jewelry to textiles to various assorted antiquities. That day, however, we wanted to just get acquainted. A trip upstairs to view his carpets was to come about two days later. In the meantime, through his recommendation, we arranged for a driver to take us to some wonderful archaeological sites the following day.

When we did go upstairs two days later Hassan's business partner also came along since carpets were his forte. The two of them were exchanging comments in Arabic as Diane and I began looking around. This time, a purchase was made within an hour. Did I say a runner? Well, we bought two. No need to elaborate on the purchase details, but they were complex.

It was the wonderful friendship that developed between Hassan, Diane and me over the ensuing five days that made this encounter special. We shared many, many hours of dialogue over the course of four evenings with not only him but with his partner and the mother of his son, as well as with intellectually stimulating friends. Our tastes in history, architecture, politics and so many other topics were also exchanged on long walks through the old and new cities of Aleppo. The discussions were both serious and humorous.

In the beginning of this segment, I mentioned the dialogue in Arabic between Hassan and his partner when we first bartered for a carpet. Hassan later told us that they had been heatedly discussing whether to bargain (Hassan's preference) or stick with a fixed price. For us, bargaining was more enjoyable, even though we know that merchants never lose on these "deals."

Update: February 2017

Hassan is now in Istanbul with his wife and two of his children. Two older boys are refugees in the Netherlands. Along with most of Aleppo, his store, his home and all of his belongings have been destroyed by bombs.

Via the Internet we have followed their travails. When and where to escape over the border; the refugee camps; looking for work; finding work but getting cheated repeatedly; schooling for his children; health care. The next meal. Racist remarks daily. So sad.

THE SINGING
WELL AND THE
OMELET

❖

The following account about our visit to an indigenous area in northern Kenya has features more likely to come from a creative writing class than from real life. Our trip took place in 1991 and unanticipated events took place.

In Northern Kenya, about 265 miles north of Nairobi, there is an indigenous community who tend camels, sheep, and goats. They are the Rendille tribe, and their semi-desert outpost was our destination in 1992.

My wife Diane and I were invited by our long-time friend Jean Colvin to accompany her to take Andrew, a young Rendille man, to visit his parents and family years after earning a college

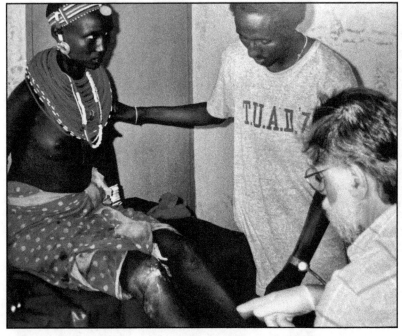

The author examinging a patient on a very hot afternoon in Kenya

degree in the United States. Missionaries in Kenya had identified him as a gifted student, so, with the financial assistance of our close friends and fellow travelers, he became the first tribesman with an education beyond high school.

Soon after arrival in Kenya, Andrew arranged for me to observe an evening meeting of the male elders who adjudicated community disputes and were responsible for significant tribal decisions. On another day, I volunteered to see some sick villagers and ended up with a patient load of about 60.

We had many memorable experiences, but the one about the Singing Well and the omelet is my favorite.

The rain was late that year, and the consequences were multiple. Crops couldn't be harvested, and the animals had to be moved many miles for grazing. We observed the herders obtaining blood from the neck veins of their camels and mixing it with the animals' milk for nutrition. With the home area water supply

Site of the Singing Well, Northern Kenya

exhausted, the women had to walk a long way every day to a regional well. It was there that we went to visit the key locale of this story.

Long before locating the well, we could hear repeated chanting that seemed to be coming from the depths of the earth. Yes, the earth was singing. And as we approached the source, we could see an assemblage of women, children, sheep, goats and the ever-present dogs.

The water well was rectangular at the top without any surface structure such as a crank and pulley. Like a theatre stage it was the center of attention, and the audience mentioned above patiently waited for its life-sustaining product.

One man was visible over this orifice in the earth. He was the top link of a chain of men braced within the deep walls of the well passing the buckets up from the bottom and down to the depths. As they worked, they sang, and hummed, and sang again. It was hypnotic.

A few days later, while I volunteered in the aforementioned clinic, Diane and our leader and friend Jean returned to what we now called "the Singing Well." On this occasion the procurement of water and the singing were the same, but the participants were different. Unlike on our first visit, the natives this time objected to any photography. An argument ensued and things were

Our goat being escorted to our camp

getting out of hand until a solution was reached.

With a generous offer for a few photos and with smiles and handshakes, a goat was purchased from the people at the well. The description of Diane and Jean placing plastic over the back seat of their Land Rover and restraining this unappreciative and uncooperative animal for the return trip was hilarious.

Later that afternoon, after a long day at the clinic, I tried resting in our tent. I was unsuccessful because of the incessant crying just outside. When I lifted the tent flap, I saw the upset goat tied to a nearby tree. A few minutes later Diane explained to me in detail about their morning adventure.

Soon thereafter the elders convened and quickly made two decisions. First, our recently purchased goat was taken to the area where other goats grazed, and the crying stopped.

Then we experienced decision number two. The elders knew we intended to give the goat to them, and they appreciated our generosity. In return they arranged for the entire community to benefit from the gift. That evening the slaughtered goat was grilled and shared.

Early the next morning our group was treated to a unique treat – a vegetable omelet with roasted goat. There is a good reason why one rarely sees goat listed as an option in Bay Area restaurants.

A postscript: Andrew went on to get his doctorate at U.C. Berkeley and he now works for the World Bank with key administrative responsibility in Africa.

EN ROUTE

❖

West African travel has been a challenge since the beginning of time. This is still true in our 21st century. West Africa is an area of the world from which many slaves came to America. Today many of its countries are struggling to provide education and economic stability. Travel and tourism can be a challenge in this region. For instance, below is an account of a 24-hour period in which we were traveling from The Gambia to Mali via Senegal.

We have finally settled in Segou, Mali, thoroughly enjoying the 6th annual Festival on the Niger. None of the "firsts" that occurred en route deserve much mention individually, but since they all happened within 14 hours, they collectively support the phrase that "Getting there is half the fun."

1. After settling down on Air Senegal Flight v201 from Banjul, The Gambia to Dakar, Senegal I looked up at that screen that the planes

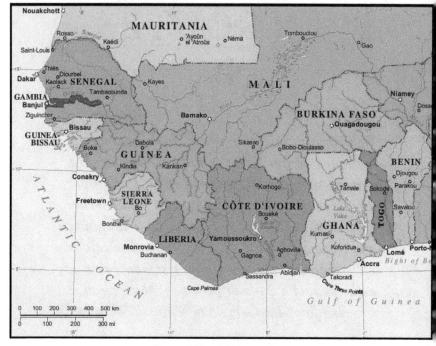

Map of North West Africa
(Courtesy of Research Gate)

have that show a plane image going from point A to point B. We were not heading for Dakar but to Conakry, Guinea.

2. On our way out of our hotel the next morning to be at the airport by 0600 we could not leave the second-floor hotel because all the doors were locked, and nobody was around.

3. Despite having tickets in hand and both phone and email confirmation of our Dakar to Bamako, Mali flight on Aerienne du Mali airline,

106

the ticket agent refused to let us on because our tickets were not electronic. We had to pay cash for two one-way tickets.

4. At the Dakar airport the arrival area had a band, military guard, red carpet and a throng of people. Of course, not for us. The special reception was for the next flight.

5. I needed to do a cash advance transaction at the Bamako bank to get money for tours, etc., as credit cards do not work here. During the transaction process the woman bank officer handed me a gift in a bag. It was a roll of toilet paper that turned out to be a great gift.

WELCOME TO DETROIT

❖

Their real names are not Danilo, Rosauro and Malea. I think it is best to use pseudonyms. I first heard about their August 2005 Detroit adventure sipping a mojito with Danilo (again, not his real name) while touring Cuba in 2012.

Rosauro repeatedly checked the bulge inside his coat jacket just to make sure the nine thousand Canadian dollars was still there. Next to him on Northwest Flight 771 was his wife, Malea. She securely held the purse in her lap that contained the stub of her boarding pass, lipstick, some mints, tissue, the treasured Canadian visa documents for both of them, and her passport. Oh yes, and the thick envelope with a similar ninety Canadian one-hundred-dollar bills. Her older brother Danilo was sitting just across the aisle dozing off. His nine thousand was somewhere close. For security reasons they had decided to each share a third.

Their final destination was Toronto, where fourteen years earlier Danilo had successfully become a citizen and where Malea and Rosauro now planned to settle.

Three days earlier the couple had withdrawn twenty-seven thousand dollars (their life savings) from the Metropolitan Bank in Manila and insisted on cash. They made sure to have a letter from the bank that assured any reader that the money was legitimately withdrawn, and it even had the serial numbers listed.

Danilo and Malea have always been quite close. Their Chinese father and Filipino mother had a small business near Manila, and they grew up in a modest home. They paid cash for everything. In fact, only Danilo used a credit card, and only after he moved to the U.S. and then Canada, where he became a successful, hard-working accountant.

Malea has a business degree. While in school she met Rosauro and they married soon after he received his mechanical engineering diploma. Together they sequestered their savings for five or six years with the intention of joining Danilo someday in Toronto and starting a new life. Flight 771 was headed first to Detroit, and then, after a five-hour layover, to this new opportunity in Toronto. The $27,000 would help obtain housing, a car, and other essentials once they got there.

We have all seen the traditional U.S. Customs form that is handed to us en route to the States. The part about declaring if we have $10,000 or more in our possession comes from the Currency and Foreign Transaction Reporting Act. It states: "… You may legally carry any amount of money into or out of the U.S., but if it is more than $10,000 at any one time, you must report it or risk U.S. Customs taking it and never getting it back, because failure to report it is a violation of the Currency and Foreign Transaction Reporting Act. The passenger(s) carrying the money must file a FinCEN Form 105 at the time of entry

Signage on luggage carts at the Detroit airport

into the U.S." The purpose of this second form is to determine proof of the legitimate source of the money and proof of its intended use.

All of this is spelled out on the backside of the initial sheet completed by all passengers.

The flight from Manila to Detroit took more than seventeen hours. Obviously a very fatiguing journey under any circumstances; nevertheless, there was plenty of time to discuss the customs form question with their answer. Since Malea and Rosauro had documentation from the Manila bank showing the legal withdrawal of the money and even the serial numbers on the currency, they decided that simply declaring "yes" to the inquiry about money and handing the form to the customs agent in Detroit would suffice. Any other required documentation could come later. They never bothered to inquire about FinCEN Form 105 from the flight attendants. In fact, they paid little attention to the back of the initial form.

After a long walk through endless corridors at Detroit Metropolitan Wayne County Airport, the first stop was the Immigration booth labeled "Non-U.S. Citizens." A middle-aged Immigration agent with a crew cut inspected their Canadian visa documents plus passports and with a quick wave of his hand told them to follow the blue line on the floor to Customs.

It was Danilo who handed the form that they had filled out and signed about ten hours earlier to the Customs agent. After a quick glance he told all three to identify their luggage and to step aside. Two other agents then removed every article of clothing and each and every other item from their bags. They prodded, patted, and poked for any concealed pockets. Finding nothing suspicious, the contents were replaced haphazardly into each suitcase. Without further discussion or explanation, they were then escorted to a nearby room and ordered to turn over all their money.

For the next three hours two agents took turns asking them where they were going, why, and made them repeat over and over how the $27,000 was obtained. Danilo demanded that they return the money because they had not done anything illegal and had simply been totally honest when completing the form. The agents said they understood this but, in the end, the agents kept the money and handed them Form DET-CMI-II (REV 111202). It was seven pages long and single-spaced.

Form DET-CMI-II included a notice of seizure of currency, election of proceedings, seized asset claimed form, proof of legitimate source and use, and an explanation of their legal options. Their seized funds would be kept for 30 days in a vault and if no petition for return was filed in that time frame, they would never see any of their money again.

Soon after arriving in Toronto Danilo sought the advice of a customs attorney. For $4000 paid in advance an expedited appeal could be filed on a "no promises" basis.

Acceptance meant that now Danilo was dipping into his own savings. He did not believe he had any other option. The lawyer's work on the case was minimal because the three of them did not need to obtain or provide any more documentation for the seized asset claim form than they had already had in their possession back in Detroit.

Seventy-two days after their horrible experience in Detroit they received a check from the U.S. Treasury. That is, minus $2500 for what Customs labeled a "mitigated forfeiture fee." In addition to the loss of $6500 (forfeiture and attorney fees) they were required to sign a Hold Harmless Agreement. Translated, this means they agreed not to sue U.S. Customs.

EPILOGUE

My research for this story revealed that in order for any money to be seized, there has to be evidence that the person or persons had knowledge of the reporting requirement and knowingly failed to report it (possession of >$10,000).

Danilo, Malea and Rosauro certainly had knowledge of the requirement and appropriately checked off "yes" on the form. It appears that their "sin" was not filling out FinCEN Form 105 prior to arriving at Customs in Detroit.

Based on my reading multiple similar case reports, it appears that U.S. Customs personnel have the discretion to be helpful and assist passengers when they fail to provide a completed FinCEN Form 105. Or, depending on jurisdiction, knowledge may not be a requirement for seizure by Customs.

I asked Danilo why they did not fly directly from Manila to Toronto. Flying via Detroit was much cheaper, at least they thought.

My thanks to Danilo (you know who I mean) for giving me your time in retelling this painful and expensive travel adventure.

March 2012

Reference: Customs and International Trade Law Blog, Feb. 2010

BARGAINING PLUS A BONUS

❖

I suppose people who lived in caves bartered for goods. There's no evidence that Adam and Eve did it, but perhaps they should have. In the Western world it is mostly done in flea markets and second-hand stores. The story below includes our experiences in Morocco and India.

In many continents over three decades, and may it never end, every experience is remembered as if it took place just last week.

The experience is entering a souk or bazaar with the intent to buy. I have chosen scenes that took place in Morocco and India.

Initially I was intimidated by the souks. The eyes of merchants catching your entry into their small sphere of influence is felt. A glance their way is interpreted as permission to cast their line for the fish. And we are the fish! Surrounding us

Watching the crowd

are the serpentine alleyways with foreign sounds, aromas and the unexpected. These bazaars and souks seemingly place me on the set of a foreign movie with 1001 characters milling about like agitated bees in a hive.

A significant, calming, and reassuring transition happens when one leaves the milieu of uncertainty mentioned above and enters a merchant's shop within the bazaar or souk. Particularly, if it is your intention to make a purchase. No longer are you the fish in the ocean; no longer is the scene foreign with so much apparent Brownian movement. In a way, outside you were an extra in that movie; now you become a principal character. This is the intention of the merchant, and he facilitates the fantasy well. No popcorn today, but may I offer the reader a cup

The Aleppo Souk – demolished two years subsequent to photo by bombs

of mint tea and the following:

In 1983, we made our first visit to Morocco. A trip through the souk there is a must. Diane wanted to purchase some Berber jewelry for her shop in San Francisco so there we were around 10:00 A.M. in Fez, sipping tea while sitting on beautiful carpets on the third floor of a gracious merchant's shop. He chatted with us while three assistants progressively brought out more stunning pieces for our inspection. Diane had a spending limit, and the merchant, of course, had a price limit.

On and on the process went, with counter offers and the switching of candidate jewelry. After three hours and lots of tea, the exchange was finalized. A djellaba for me was also thrown in. But that was not the end. The merchant hugged us both, congratulated us for choosing such quality and being so astute in bargaining and proceeded to invite us to his home. It was around 10:00 P.M., twelve hours after first entering his shop, when we left. His wife had prepared two separate meals for us all while we watched videos of their recent wedding. The entire wedding celebration lasted a week.

In 2000 we returned to Morocco and a rental house in the Marrakesh medina. For centuries this region of the city has been like no other in the world except perhaps for the medina in Fez. Its epicenter is called Jemaa el-Fna and it is over-populated with peddlers, scammers, henna hand painters and tourists. One particular individual caught my attention as we were exiting the souk. A long snake was wrapped around his shoulders, and in less than 10 seconds it was slithering on my shoulders. Very soon people were gathering to observe the spectacle. I pleaded with Diane to give the snake owner a tip to remove it. She complied – well, sort of. Only after making sure she got some photos. "Look at me and smile!"

It was 2000 and warm that afternoon in Jodhpur, India when Diane and I took a taxi to buy bedspreads in the central bazaar. I had trouble exiting the taxi because a cow was standing right outside my car door. The whole area was crowded with families looking at what the street vendors were showing, and it took us a while to find a merchant with the proper selections.

Shortly thereafter we were sipping tea on the second floor while sitting atop a three-foot-high assemblage of carpets, listening to the owner describe the benefits of various choices of stunning bedspreads that his three assistants were displaying.

It rhymes — The smile is a fake because of the snake

To this day I am still uncertain if what then ensued was spontaneous or designed. I will never know, and it doesn't matter.

We liked one particular bedspread, but the price of this one plus one other was too high. After offering some unacceptable alternatives the store owner asked me, "What can I offer you for your lovely wristwatch?" I was momentarily speechless but soon told him that it was a fake Rolex that I had purchased for less than $10 that year in Hanoi. He said he did not care because such watches are not available in Jodhpur. After telling him "No," I thought a bit and quickly

Nuts are always a favorite in the Moroccan Souk

changed my mind. I decided that I really did not have any particular affection for that timepiece.

Off came the watch and the owner lowered his price, and the most charming scene then occurred in that showroom. I looked up and the owner was admiring his new watch (the fake Rolex) while his first assistant proudly put on the owner's now former wristwatch. The next assistant acquired the first assistant's and so on. The room was full of four men with new watches and us with the bedspreads we wanted. Just another day at the bazaar.

THE ELUSIVE TIGER

On multiple occasions we have visited India's national parks for wonderful bird watching and hunting (with cameras and binoculars) for tigers.

It is very interesting to watch the guides and drivers on a safari when there is a tiger or elephants nearby. There is silence, keen watchfulness, and anticipation. There exists a deep sense of respect for these wonders of the animal kingdom.

In India there are great efforts to save the tigers from extinction; poachers are the problem.

Diane and I have been to five national parks during our two six-week visits to India. Wild elephants we have seen and admired greatly. But oh, those elusive tigers.

We have been close. Twice the squawking of birds and monkeys has told us that a tiger is nearby. And leaning out of Jeeps we have seen fresh paw prints on three or four occasions. Frustrating also was the fact that others had sighted the mighty tiger only a few minutes before.

And so, on this particular adventure Diane and I were in a national park called Simlipal, about 350 km southwest of Kolkata, knowing that there were tigers there but also having been advised that they are deep in the bush and seldom seen.

A full day in the park was about to end and we had a tough five-hour Jeep ride back to our cabin. Our guide said we should stop and get out and wait near this particular road crossing as the sun set because it was a well-known elephant corridor, and we might be lucky and see a herd pass. After scanning the forest and watching for signs of movement, or even the sound of those mighty beasts as they crash through the forest, I noticed tracks in the dirt road. Paw prints. Many of them, and they were fresh. The thought of getting back into the Jeep for protection entered

Image of tiger print
(Courtesy of Etsy; designed by Divine Burn)

my mind. I showed the prints to Diane and she, too, became excited. Our first tiger sighting? Finally, after all the recent frustration!

And then we burst out laughing. A real, hilarious, ten out of ten, shared laugh that captured so much in ten seconds that we will remember it forever.

Why? Because we realized that we were looking at the impressions left by the heel of Diane's boot.

Tiger viewed on subsequent trip to India

HLUHLUWE

❖

For most Westerners South Africa means national parks and safaris. So it was with us, but with three weeks of wandering around the country we experienced much more. A week after enjoying Kruger National Park with expert guides the two of us explored Hluhluwe on our own. I believe this story could not have happened with more people. It is one of my all-time favorites.

When looking at Hluhluwe one would never pronounce it "Shloo-Shloo-Wee" unless they knew Zulu. The location for this story is Hluhluwe-Imfolozi Park in South Africa and on this particular mid-summer day it is hot. So hot that the animals are hidden and subdued; so hot that most other humans are hidden, subdued or around air conditioners. And so hot that Diane and I are tucked beneath the only shade tree that we could find on the dirt road we are driving on in the park. Our intent is to view birdlife and hopefully other inhabitants of the area. Only two days earlier we saw a large rhino as well as a huge elephant along a nearby road in this same sector. But they were seen in the late afternoon when the sun was less intense.

This part of South Africa is called KwaZulu-Natal, and its landscape is simply stunning. Our car is parked on a slight promontory and for miles and miles the sky is blue with only a few white splotches of cumulus. The hills all around seem to just undulate and roll and are without sharp edges. Every variety of tree (fever, acacia, ironwood, thorn, etc.) seems to be there for a specific purpose. Sometimes for food, sometimes for shade, sometimes just for a bird to rest on. And in the distance, as far as the eye can see, way out there where the sky bows down to touch the earth, there is a sea of green. For it is summer and the rains have come. The tall grasses of South Africa, just like the waters of our oceans, provide food and shelter. The impalas prance through it, and the lions hide in it.

On that hot afternoon our search for things exotic was only somewhat successful. A tree full of baboons and some new bird sightings provided some entertainment. But we, too, were hot, wet with perspiration, and tired. So it was under that tree in the shade that we did what we

Our fellow nappers — note red billed oxpecker on face of giraffe

both were quite accomplished at. We took a nap.

Perhaps it was thirty minutes later. Maybe more. Whoever awakened first whispered "Wow!" and both of us for a long, long time just looked, and marveled, and looked some more and appreciated. They were all in front of us and we had front row orchestra seats.

At stage left, a very young giraffe was lying down, which is uncommon. Standing adjacent to it was an adult female giraffe, presumably the mother. Another giraffe was standing stage right, very, very close to our car. None of the three were eating. No munching. All had red-billed oxpecker birds parading around their limbs, their torsos and even in their ears, freeing the huge hosts of their insects. The giraffes had to know we were very near, yet they simply showed no concern.

In the middle of this scene were three Burchell's or plains zebras. They are the kind who have darker "shadow stripes" superimposed on their white stripes. Their postures and attitudes clued us in to what was happening on that beautiful promontory in their home territory. They stood quietly abreast of one another, alternating face to butt to face with swishing tails serving as fans and fly repellants.

The three giraffes and three zebras had come to this little rise, with its bit of clearing, to also take naps. A slight breeze made the tall green grass move like cilia, and the zebra tails swished. The giraffes stood still, and we watched in silence.

For about thirty minutes we absorbed this stillness, and then decided to leave. Our first concern was starting the motor. Done without a stir. Then the crawl forward beneath the semi arc formed by the front of the giraffe on the right. Again, no change.

As our car tiptoed out of that "bedroom" I

recalled doing the same thing over thirty years ago. Many times, I cherished watching the serenity of sleep of Adam, Sarah, Molly or Aniwa. And above their cribs hung a mobile with giraffes and zebras and other inhabitants of South Africa.

Giraffe with red-billed oxpecker just outside my car window

Part Two

*A few collected memories that
are not travel related*

When a one month old boy taught me
a practical lesson.

How ten of us were the second group in
the country to start a fantasy football league.

A five-week murder trial in which I was
a jury foreman. Over and over the concept of
reasonable doubt had to be explained.

THE FOUNTAIN
OF YOUTH

❖

The following adventure took place in 1968 during the beginning of my third year at Albany Medical School. By that time most of my classmates were married with infants and were well trained in child care. I was single with no recent or past history of the handling and management of babies.

S o with this introduction, let's begin with my first real clinical introduction to direct patient care. I was moving out of the classroom and lab, and was about to deal with real patients. Nervous? A bit, but I was looking forward to the new experience. The assignment was for me to be in the Pediatric Well Baby Clinic where I would interview the mother, examine the one-month-old infant, and give advice.

To prepare us, the faculty advisor demonstrated how to ask pertinent questions from the mother (or grandmother), the recommended sequencing and methodology of the exam, what to look for, and then what advice to be prepared to give.

The setting was a long, narrow room with one side having multiple cubicles for the exams. Separating each area were walls that did not extend to the ceiling. In the area there usually were about four infants being examined simultaneously.

So there I am on this fateful morning with a baby boy laying on his back on the exam table. While I was briefly glancing at the baby and talking to his mother, a loud, angry scream emanated from the adjacent cubicle.

It was at that moment that I learned to always cover a male infant's privates with a loose diaper during an exam. On that morning my little patient had accomplished a feat that resulted in a high arced powerful stream of urine passing up and over the cubicle wall onto a nearby unsuspecting mother.

So often the things one learns in medical school do not originate in the classroom or textbooks. Thanks to that little fellow for a valuable and practical example.

58
CONSECUTIVE
YEARS OF
FANTASY
FOOTBALL

❖

Below is my personal experience with fantasy football, including many of the so-called "trimmings." When I first participated in 1972 it had only one or two years of very minimal participation and quite often our participants made up their own rules and formats. Nowadays fantasy sports make up a huge sports exercise with many, many high-income experts getting paid to guess football performances.

Fantasy Football leagues are now common in all types of work settings, in our newspapers, on the Internet and more. With a few clicks here and a few clicks there, anyone can become a coach. The menu options include varieties such as standard draft leagues going "head-to-head" or "total points." There are spinoffs such as auction draft leagues, dynasty, keeper, and survivor varieties, to name a few.

An NFL game today need not be close to generate interest. Any fantasy coach with a player or defense still involved will pay attention even if the score is 41 to 10.

The new 1.1-billion-dollar stadium built by the San Francisco 49ers has sophisticated Wi-Fi and an app designed so the fans in the stadium can follow "live" the performances of their fantasy players around the country. There is also a Fantasy Football Lounge onsite with over fifty televisions that are devoted to providing live performance updates of individual NFL players. One T.V. screen for EACH player!

Back in the late 60s when the late Tom Canepa started our league, the situation was very different. Think primitive. Think unknown territory. The term "Fantasy Football," for instance, had not even been hatched. Tom and his son Gordon established the framework, and it was called simply "the football pool." Tom got the basics from a San Francisco Balboa High School coach. After a year in that pool Tom and his son Gordon established their own league. Today it is called the Tom Canepa Memorial Fantasy League.

Bob, a coworker, and I joined the pool in 1972. In 1978 an attorney friend of Bob thought the idea had such great potential that he recommended we apply for a copyright. Bob dismissed the idea saying, "Nobody would be crazy enough to do this but our group."

When I mentioned to (Tom's son) Gordon that I was going to write this story he quickly reeled off one of his early "pool" rosters. (Based on his team's 2023 performance, I think Gordon wants these guys back.) That roster included:

Roman Gabriel
Sonny Jurgensen
Leroy Kelly
Gino Cappelletti
O.J. Simpson
Larry Csonka
Bob Hayes
Paul Warfield
Jack Snow
Preston Pearson
Don Maynard

Selected Memories

… And last, but not least, Pete Gogolak.

A lot of this story or account will be the "back thens." For instance, back then there were no fantasy experts providing cheat sheets, sleeper lists or draft strategies. Nothing. Zilch. A coach was on his own to search for any weekly hints.

To think that hundreds of people are now paid thousands to prognosticate via T.V. and websites about NFL players and teams is mind-boggling. With the advent of the Internet, coupled with the explosion of Fantasy partici-pants, this collection of experts was launched.

For many years our key source of information on players came from Pro Football magazines that showed up around late June. At our draft we all seemed to rely on the same reference lists from those magazines. The information on teams and players by Sports Illustrated and similar pe-riodicals was useless. What they concentrated on was not what the fantasy coach needed.

My very first rookie "pool" mistake cost me a lot of points. At a pre-season 49er game I saw a Seattle wide receiver make incredible catches, so a few weeks later I selected him in our draft. In the regular season he barely made it into any game. Most likely by mid-season he was selling used Edsels. From that time on I have ignored pre-season game performances. More misleading than helpful.

Remember the typewriter? It was our sole instrument to record and distribute rosters.

In 1980 on a December Sunday morning, I called a former classmate who resided in Buffalo.

"Hi Art, how are you? How's the family and kids?" I asked.

"Gee, so nice of you to call. We're fine."

I then asked, "How are you holding out in that Buffalo weather?"

"Pretty well. A big storm is coming in, but not until late this afternoon."

Aha!! Mission accomplished. After chatting a bit more I hung up and called in my picks that included Joe Cribbs, the Buffalo Bills running back, who had a great game prior to the Buffalo storm.

Back then you had no idea what the weather was like at game time around the country.

I mentioned calling in one's picks. That was the only way to make your weekly choices, and each week you had to declare your selections via phone by 9:59 Sunday morning. Ideally a bit earlier, because at that time all the other coaches would tend to be on the line.

None of us were ardent about religion but sometimes Gordon or his dad went to church on Sunday around 10:00 A.M. That left their wives with the task of marking our called-in picks with accompanying questions such as, "How do you spell Biletnikoff or Starbauch?"

On one particular Monday, I still had the opportunity to choose between two running backs for that evening's game. Because Gordon was still at work, I called Tom a few minutes before kickoff to declare my choice, only to be told by his wife that he was quite busy with a "call of nature." Add this situation of natural disasters to the likes of floods, fires, and earthquakes.

Sunday-only games made things easier. There were no bye weeks and fewer teams. Now we have the addition of Monday, Thursday and sometimes Saturday games.

Ah, yes, Monday night football with Howard Cosell, Don Meredith, Frank Gifford and the rest. A different type of entertainment. For instance, I remember one Monday when two guests dominated the third quarter while Howard Cosell periodically paid attention to the two teams down below. Their guests were Ronald Reagan and John Lennon. On the air Mr. Reagan was trying to explain the basics of the game to the famous Beatle while we tried to determine if our running backs and others were scoring points for us.

Injuries are part of the game. Teams and

coaches also "game" the injuries. Today the NFL oversees the various injury lists to try and make them honest, timely and legitimate. This was not the case in the past. We had to try and rely on the "official" Wednesday injury information published in the Thursday paper and it was as reliable as the weather report from the Philippines.

Too often a midweek healthy Art Monk or Jerome Bettis would be limping and inactive come Sunday and it would be too late to make a roster change. NFL coaches back then purposely withheld information regarding a player's status.

Obtaining the game results via radio or T.V. late on Sunday was seldom a problem, but forget about any individual stats. A running back or wide receiver going over 100 yards was not a particularly newsworthy event. We had to rely on the Monday morning San Francisco Chronicle for our data. Sometimes I would pre-empt the process by driving down to the corner of Van Ness and Geary between 10:00 and 10:30 on Sunday night to intercept the Chronicle delivery truck when it arrived at the corner vending machine.

On Tuesday Tom and Gordon, as "official league recorders," would tally the results of each fantasy coach using the Chronicle data. Any disputes such as discovering a mistake by the Chronicle would be handled by our commissioner.

Gordon still serves that function, but disputes are now rare.

The waiver wire spoils fantasy participants. Nowadays the Internet allows this weekly process to take place effortlessly. The same with trades, if your league includes them. For over 25 years we did not have such a luxury. After the original pre-season draft a coach had only one opportunity to drop players who were injured, waived or in jail (not that rare an occurrence). This opportunity was called the mid-season draft. For the second half of the season your roster was again set in stone.

Some fantasy leagues are big money events. Not for us. From its inception our group has preferred bragging rights over dollars. Recently we added a meaningful last place prize. A battered, half-deflated old football with bladder problems. Some similarity there to the older coaches!

Other fantasy leagues in the country have some brutal consequences for coming in last. In one New Jersey league the first-place coach gets to select the tattoo image that the last-place coach must accept. There is a YouTube clip of such an event where the poor loser is getting the face of Justin Bieber inked into his thigh.

In another East Coast league, the loser must apply for, take and publish the results of that year's college SAT tests.

**A battered, half-deflated old football
with bladder problems**

Rule changes evolved over the years. Initially
we made our own because there were few other
models to emulate. We expanded the number of
roster positions to try and compensate for the
loss of players that could not be replaced until

mid-season. Defensive scores came only from resultant immediate touchdowns because the recording of sacks, fumbles and interceptions was inconsistent. PPR (point per reception) was introduced about twenty years ago.

We must be doing something right because our coaches tend to re-enlist every year to brag, moan and await the next kickoff. Explaining it all to someone who has never heard of Fantasy Football is quite a task. What does it all mean? It seems to take up a lot of your time, they say.

It is indeed hard to rationalize, but so is the game itself, with 325-pound Neanderthals struggling to control a little bag of air.

WHO SHOT
SUZIE Q

This is a lengthy story, but so was the trial. Over five weeks. I have changed the names of the participants for obvious reasons. Every evening during the trial I went to my notes (allowed by the judge) and laid out my observations and described the testimony. There were many boring moments during this trial, and this is obvious when you read it, but I chose to pretty much write it down without much editing or revisions.

I t was not Suzie Q who was murdered. It was Wai Sook Lee. But Harry Norton called her Suzie Q since he had trouble with names. She was shot three times. Died for sure from the first bullet. We'll get to her and Harry later.

The courtroom, officially known as Department 21, is located on the third-floor corner of a San Francisco building that would fit well into the landscape of old Russian-occupied Bucharest. Large volume, multipurpose buildings such as this do not have to be gray with harsh corners and interiors without imagination, but so be it.

Of course one must pass through a security check. On day one of this adventure the morning line for the process extended out the door and about 100 yards down the block. Those waiting with me to be screened were an eclectic bunch. Some were well-dressed. Others, less so. I could read stress on a few faces. Two women in particular caught my attention. They were conversing with one another while talking to someone else on their cell phones. They were at least twenty feet apart, talking loudly both on the phone and to each other, and every sentence included at least one "motherfucker." When I eventually got to the front of the line, I was told that one of the security guards had "called in sick." The budget crisis did not allow for substitution.

Room 307, the Juror Assembly Room, despite its large clock without hands and the broken chairs, is at least unique for a public room at 850 Bryant in that it has windows. That's the good news. Just outside one set of windows sit eight lanes of congested traffic to and from our Bay Bridge. The windows on the west side face the jail, with its smoked glass facade. Nevertheless,

San Francisco Hall of Justice, Dept. 21
Site of trial

over the course of the next five weeks I would seek out this area for a place to read and sometimes have a sandwich.

Three groups with at least seventy-five prospective jurors were to be screened for this trial. I was in the first herd. Judge Carson, whom I would progressively come to admire for his sensitivity and professionalism, told us not to be concerned about the bulletproof glass separating the spectator area from the courtroom. He added that this trial was a robbery-murder case that would take approximately five weeks to complete. The first phase for selection would be for him to talk to anyone who had a significant reason why they could not serve for the anticipated time or those who had a hearing or English comprehension problem. The rest of us were excused and told to return in two days.

When I returned for the subsequent selection phase I swept through the security portal sans cell phone and loose change. Unlike at airports, my metal total hip replacement was not detected. Hmmm.

Judge Carson started by having Sophia, the clerk, read off to us the list of people who would testify. Then a series of questions followed, including some specifics of the robbery-murder – the names of those robbed, the names of the murder victim and the accused. Did we know any of these people? Did we have prior knowledge of the case? For the prospective jurors who advanced there were individual questions from the attorneys. Some candidates were excused because of their responses. When I progressed from being a groupie to the individual interview, I felt quite confident. In the past I had always been eliminated at this point. Mr. Addison, the defense attorney, looked at me and said, "Doctor, I have a sore elbow." At least this was somewhat unique. Most jokesters usually mention low backs or knees. Counsel Hallinan, the prosecutor, asked me why some people lie. There was nothing unique to my answer.

I tried to figure out what the strategy of both sides was for juror selection or elimination.

It seemed to me that the defense did not want Asians. This made sense to me because, after all, the victims were Korean. Somebody else suggested that obvious gays were also excused.

Perhaps. In any event, after both sides each eliminated over twenty people, I became Juror Number 9.

Up until this point, I was more or less passive. Just a spectator. As the judge swore us in, he told us that we were not to discuss any aspects of the case with significant others, even insignificant others, and that we were not to visit the crime scene neighborhood, not to search for information on the Internet or from any source – and perhaps he gave other instructions, but my mind paradoxically now was both numb and active. Jesus, this is real. Oh yes, and until all the evidence was presented, no trial discussions amongst jurors.

Taking life away from another has gradations. Both U.S. presidential candidates said they would kill terrorists if captured. They did not even use the term "bring them to justice." Murder is commonplace in books, movies and television. The handling of death itself also has its contradictory aspects aspects. *Six Feet Under* depicts it with an "in your face" approach, but the media cannot photograph the scores of military coffins returning from Iraq. While I was thinking about these things the Judge announced that this was not a death penalty case.

THE CRIME

When I approached the security scanner the next day, I decided to see what would happen if I went through without removing coins, money clip, and my cell phone. No alarm went off to indicate metal. I mentioned my metallic total hip replacement to the officer, and he simply responded, "This ain't the airport." I guess he had me with that comment.

After the Judge again went over our instructions (assimilate only the evidence presented and do not discuss anything) he read the definition of "reasonable doubt." We would hear that again and again later.

We were there to determine whether a young man had murdered a store co-owner and neighbor in their San Francisco Visitacion Valley neighborhood. That area has characteristics seen in parts of all large cities, in which employed, low-income residents strive against high odds to survive. Attempts to pay the bills and enjoy a satisfying quality of life are offset by many obstacles, including substance abuse, crime, and general neglect by their city leaders. Wandering the streets and hanging out on corners are poorly motivated youth and unemployed, bored young men seeking a free cigarette, joint or alcohol. It was in this scenario that the prosecuting attorney told us about the crime.

At around 8:00 A.M. on the morning of April 3, 1999, Mr. and Mrs. Lee had opened their grocery store at the corner of Wilde Avenue and Rutland Street in Visitacion Valley. They had put about $50 in small bills into the cash register to start the day, and prior to 9:00 A.M. only a few customers had come in for small purchases.

At approximately 9:10 that morning, a black man wearing gloves and a dark gray ski mask with eyeholes entered the front door of this KC Market. In his right hand was a gun which he waved in the air, and he shouted, "Give me money and Hennessy whiskey." He then threw a bag that he had brought with him over the counter, and he followed by hurtling himself over the same counter toward Mrs. Lee and the cash register. Mr. Lee, who was standing in front near the counter but to the side, told his wife, "Give him what he wants and get him out of here." According to Mr. Lee, his wife scooped the cash (singles, fives, and tens) out of the register and placed them into the bag, which was on the floor. Mr. Lee said in later testimony that he thought the bag was beige in color. Mrs. Lee then turned around and removed many Hennessy cognac bottles that were displayed in three sizes on the shelves just behind the register. The robber assisted her and together they put the bottles into his bag. After all of the Hennessy bottles were removed, Mrs. Lee then walked along the counter aisle toward the door and opened a swinging counter door to assist him with his exit. He passed by her and then, when he was between the store door and the counter, he turned around and at point blank range fired three to four shots into her. As the robber fled, Mr. Lee went to his wife and cradled her in his arms and called 911. While he was making the call Amin Ahmad, the adult son of the former store owner, came into the store for a brief moment and then left.

After hearing this description, the jury was then shown a police crime scene videotape taken that fateful Saturday morning. We saw the

Crime Scene neighborhood
Intersection Wilde Ave. and Rutland St.,
Harkness Ave. is at end of Rutland St. in the distance.

exterior of the store, including a small portion of adjacent Rutland St., and many views of the store interior with its non-functioning security camera, the counter area, and the shelves that had earlier held the Hennessy bottles. Police officers and their familiar yellow tape were also visible.

We were told that the gun used in the murder was never found.

At the trial Mr. Lee testified and everyone listened carefully. In fact, nobody in the courtroom coughed or even made shuffling noises. I thought of a lot of the small-time grocery owners I've encountered in my life. None of them are wealthy, each and every one of them putting in over 10 hours a day. The Lees had bought this store within the past year. It was clean, well-stocked and even had a new and enlarged refrigerated section.

"As much as I try to forget everything that happened, that morning is clear in my mind," Mr.Lee said via a court-appointed Korean interpreter. He sat with a straight back, wore a tie over a green shirt, his black shoes were scuffed but his white socks clean. Many questions were asked of him and a few times he suddenly rose from his seat and walked around the courtroom to help demonstrate the distances between him, his wife and the murderer on that morning. The judge allowed this unrestricted movement.

This trial took place five years and eight months after the crime. The reasons for the delay were never mentioned. It's hard for any person to remember details like color of clothes, times of day and the sequencing of events. Throughout the trial we and the many witnesses who testified would be exposed to segments of previously taped interviews they gave earlier concerning the crime. This was true for Mr. Lee. He was reminded that on April 9, 1999, four days after the murder, he told the police that the robber was "a very black man who was wearing a two-colored jacket which had yellow sleeves and a green torso." Mr. Lee was asked by the prosecuting attorney if Mrs. Lee said anything to him during the robbery. He responded affirmatively and told something to the interpreter that appeared to be difficult to translate. He wrote something in Korean on the poster pad provided by the court. The best translation was "Boo/Soaling Hahn Sah Kahm" or "A pitiable person." We learned that Mrs. Lee said this in her native tongue, and that they would turn out to be her last words. A bit later, on cross examination, we learned that it was not until September 2004 that Mr. Lee told the police about these last words from his wife.

THE HIJACKING

The jury then heard about the experiences of the Lees around a hijacking on April 1, 1999, two days before the robbery and murder. On that day Ms. Rona, a customer, came into the store and was very upset because her car, which had been parked outside, had been hijacked. We were further informed that on that evening a man named Clint Britten was caught, identified, arrested, booked and jailed for that crime.

The day after the hijacking, police inspectors performed a routine crime interview of Mrs. Lee in her store. We were told by the inspectors that Mrs. Lee told them she knew nothing about the hijacking. The police said that a young black male was in the store during the questioning, but they never identified him.

That same day, April 2, 1999, Mrs. Lee received a phone call at the store from the man who had been arrested for the hijacking. He was calling from the jail. According to Mr. Lee, she told the caller that she did not tell the police anything because she knew nothing. Nevertheless, after hanging up the phone she was, according to Mr. Lee, very, very upset.

Again, that same day, a young black man came into the store and told Mrs. Lee that it was his friend who was in jail for the hijacking. We were never told if she knew his name or what exactly was said between them.

From the cross examination by Mr. Addison, the defense attorney, the jury heard from Mr. Lee that he had always thought that the defendant Kris Davis was both the man arrested for the hijacking and the murderer of his wife. For many years he had been upset because Kris was not charged and prosecuted for the robbery and murder.

THE BAILIFF

Golly, when I progressed through the metal detecting portal the next morning the buzzer went off. Removing my belt took care of it. When I informed the security person about my passing through cleanly the day before with the same amount of metal he said, "There's always the first time." O.K., no more comments about the front door security system.

The large courthouse with its activities and employees reminded me of the surgical operating rooms where I spent my career. Serious stuff, often sad and tragic, goes on in every room and yet the workers consider it routine – because in that setting, it is. This does not tend to make one insensitive, but sometimes apathetic. Or bored. And despite the very serious nature of the business at hand, the jury did experience some light moments.

For about a month we in the jury box had to look at four desks and two tables. At the desk on the far side of the room was the bailiff, Bobby Singer. With his holster and gun and keys (two sets) and handcuffs (three sets) and radio and mace and personal protoplasmic surplus of at least 50 pounds, Lord help us if he ever had to chase anyone. He was always in our field of vision. And without fail, every morning and afternoon he would fall asleep. Right in the middle of the court activity! And we in the jury would take note because prior to the half-day proceedings we had bet on different fifteen-minute segments for this to occur.

THE DEFENDANT

Every day of the trial Kris Davis sat at the defense table. A light-skinned black man in his twenties, he wore dark slacks and a variety of colored "dress" T-shirts. To me, he appeared more like a student at State than a young man who has already matriculated at San Quentin. His attorney early on said he would not be testifying. That is always a defense option. We never heard about any history of education, marriage or even employment. He lived on Wilde Avenue, just up the street from the KC Market, with his mother, her boyfriend, a younger sister and younger brother.

MOTHER OF THE DEFENDANT

Mrs. Tanya Colville still lived in the same house on Wilde Avenue. Prior to her testimony she occasionally sat in the visitor section of the courtroom. She was about five feet five, conservatively dressed, and what I would describe as matronly. If one thinks of a cat with nine lives, she looked like she had been through five already. She gave the following account of April 3, 1999.

She had worked at that time at a security firm and she drove there that morning, arriving around 9:00 to 9:15. She said that Kris had slept at her house the night of April 2 and that she had spoken to him briefly on the morning of April 3, before going to work. It was her usual custom to call home when she arrived at work and this she did that morning, talking to Trina, her young teen daughter, her son Dexter and to Kris. When asked what she talked to Kris about she said she told him to get dressed and stop walking around the house in his underwear.

Around 11:30 Trina called her at work to inform her about the shooting at the store. A few minutes later Trina again called her mother and wanted her to come home. Mrs. Colville stated she did just that, and that when she arrived home at around 11:45 Kris was across the street from her home talking to a friend named Dominique Lewis. The two of them got into Mrs. Colville's car and had a conversation. Mrs. Colville said that they talked in general terms about the shooting. She then went into her house.

A short time later she left to return to work and while leaving her driveway she noticed Kris standing near the neighborhood school, which was further up Wilde Avenue, away from both the KC store and Rutland Street. She did not speak to him or try to see him.

She then stated that when she returned home from work in the early afternoon, she encountered Dominique Lewis in front of her house. He informed her that Kris had just been arrested. She immediately went toward the store, where there was still a large police presence from the morning shooting. It was there that she met two policemen. Homicide Inspectors Antonio Cappelletti and Arturo Castro informed her that they had just received permission from Kris's parole officer to inspect his (and her) home and asked her if she would accompany them. She did. Kris, meanwhile, was already in custody.

James Breivis

INSPECTORS CAPPELLETTI
AND CASTRO

I suppose if I oversaw casting for a movie and had to select two weathered, very experienced homicide cops, these two would make good candidates. They certainly have testified a lot in the past. Cappelletti would often have the answers before the questions were asked. I am not sure if in court this is an asset or a liability. He is now retired from the force but lo and behold, works as an inspector for the District Attorney's office, which is just around the corner from the courtroom. Castro, I thought, was less gruff. I liked that a Hispanic was represented this high on the force.

Back on April 3, 1999 they were partners, and when Mrs. Lee was declared dead they took over the case from the robbery detail. They had made a quick stop at the KC Market around noon and were headed back to the station when they received a call from robbery inspector Alexander Martin. They were told to return to Wilde Avenue, just down the street from both the crime scene and the home of Kris Davis, because the latter had just been pulled over along with an acquaintance and there was criminal evidence in their car. The contents of the car would be the topic of a lot of courtroom fodder. We would be hearing testimony from these two inspectors along with their associate, Inspector Bruce Donovan.

THE CORNER STORE

There was a Muni bus stop on Wilde Avenue, adjacent to the corner store. It was apparent from all the testimony that the KC Market attracted a lot of intentional as well as incidental foot traffic. This included the young men who hung out on the corner "just chillin'." We even heard that the brother of Ricardo Nevins, a key witness, had died near that corner earlier in the year and that Mrs. Lee had arranged to have his baseball cap attached to the corner telephone pole so people passing might place a donation to pay for some type of memorial, according to Mr. Nevins, who was upset on April 3 when he discovered that the hat was stolen.

RICARDO NEVINS

People acquainted with trials know there are always schedule changes and delays. We in the jury spent a lot of time sitting on the benches outside Department 21 talking not about this trial, perhaps the most important current event in our lives, but about mundane topics. As the days and then weeks went by, I developed very positive feelings about every one of my serendipitous peers. Bonding is too strong a word, but acceptance certainly applies.

Ricardo Nevins would turn out to be a very important witness, and also a problem for the prosecution, the defense, and the jury. I expect the reasons will become apparent to the reader once I elaborate. To me he appeared to be about forty years of age. He was well groomed, comfortable, and self-assured on the witness stand. This trial represented his fourth major testimony regarding his experience with Kris Davis on the morning of the murder. The jury either heard tapes or excerpts read from his first three testimonies and we were present for this, the fourth.

In April 1999 Inspectors Cappelletti and Castro did not have Ricardo Nevins on their radar screen for the Lee murder investigation when they received a call from their police colleagues that Mr. Nevins, who was in custody on another matter, wanted to talk to them about important information that he had about the Lee murder. So, on April 7, 1999, and then again in December 1999 (at the San Mateo County jail, where he was incarcerated), and again at his 2003 Grand Jury testimony, he gave the following story.

Early on that eventful morning Ricardo said he was in the neighborhood because his mother lived nearby, and he frequently looked in on her and checked his mail. A friend had dropped him off with the understanding that he would be picked up near the store "a bit later."

He cannot recall the time; he did not wear a watch. Nevertheless, he ran into Kris Davis, whom he had known "off and on," and Ricardo described him as being "upset." They were on Wilde Ave outside the store. He thought it might have been around 10:00 A.M. Ricardo told Inspectors Cappelletti and Castro twice and the Grand Jury once that Kris told him that he was "going to do Suki" (street parlance meaning to harm, perhaps kill Suki) and that Kris had showed Ricardo the hub of a gun stuck in his waistband beneath his coat. Ricardo then further testified that he tried to talk Kris out of it because Suki was a nice person.

Subsequently we heard, both from direct testimony by the Inspectors as well as from the original tapes, that the police were not offering Ricardo any deals regarding his fate for such testimony. Inspector Cappelletti insists that Mr. Nevins was not in drug withdrawal during the first testimony.

In the courtroom we learned that in April 1999 Ricardo Nevins was on parole for car burglary, cocaine possession, and possession of stolen property. He certainly was well known to the police. In fact, Inspector Cappelletti had met him while arresting his brother in the past. Furthermore, on April 3, 1999 Ricardo was a crack addict and alcoholic who lived in a room at the Geneva Hotel with a prostitute and another man who also were involved in smoking crack cocaine and drinking a lot of alcohol daily.

He told the jury that when he was arrested on April 7, 1999 for car burglary, he made up the above story because he needed to protect himself, because he had heard that both Kris Davis and Harry Norton (we will hear more about him later) had implicated him, Ricardo, in the murder of Mrs. Lee.

Under direct questioning at the trial, Ricardo Nevins told us that at the time of the Grand Jury he told his court-appointed attorney that he had lied about his previous statements, but that that attorney had told him it was "best to stick to his original story and we will work it out later." Therefore, per Ricardo, the Grand Jury heard the same story as the detectives did earlier regarding the April 3, 1999 early morning encounter between Ricardo and Kris Davis.

In court he insisted that he never saw Kris on the day of the robbery-murder, and that he must now tell the truth so he can "live with himself and his conscience." His current attorney was with him during this testimony. His appearance in court was with a grant of immunity!

HARRY NORTON

Harry Norton looks like a pimp. Wearing a suit with some shine to it, sunglasses, and a big smile, he looks like he is really pleased to have the opportunity to testify in court. And he talks and talks and talks.

Early mornings he takes his dog Mac for walks, and before 9:00 A.M. on April 3, 1999, he and Mac stopped at the KC Market to buy some cigarettes and beer. When asked if he was waited on by Mrs. Lee, he responded with a long dialogue about what a nice woman she was – "I called her Suzy Q" – and how she was so nice to Mac even though Mac, who was tied up near the front door, kept setting off the buzzer by moving in and out of the doorway. When he left the store, Mr. Norton said, he proceeded up Rutland St., where he saw a 14-year-old boy named Tucker Denton standing by the front gate of his house on Rutland St., near the store. We will subsequently hear a lot about that house and Tucker but for now Harry tells us that Tucker asked Harry for a cigarette. "I chewed him out for always asking me for things and smoking." Harry did give him two cigarettes (for a quarter!) and then testified that he and Tucker walked up Rutland St. away from the store toward the next street, which is Harkness Avenue. They then parted.

TUCKER DENTON

During one of the trial breaks, Rosie, Juror #11, tells me that once there was a warrant out for her arrest. Not sure how we got onto that topic but if anyone looked at and chatted with her, they would insist it had to be a mistake. It was. When she came into this same courthouse to clear it up, she was told it was a fishing violation. "That was strange because I have never fished in my life."

Everyone seemed to know Tucker. After his mother was murdered, he lived with his Aunt Diane and her husband, Stan Abrams (Kris's grandfather) at their house on Rutland St. He played an integral role in the happenings that occurred on the date of the crime. In the previous section we heard about his encounter with Harry Norton.

After being sworn in for testimony, Tucker

has to be reminded often to answer the questions with more than a "yup" or "uh huh." He is wearing a striped long-sleeved shirt that seems to be begging to be pressed. He seems to be enjoying his gum. After a long series of questions from the prosecutor, the following story is elicited.

Sometime early on the morning on April 3 he received a phone call from his friend and relative Kris Davis, who said, "I'm coming over." When asked what time this might have been we hear the first of his oft-repeated response, "I can't recall." Tucker waited by the front window to see Kris approach the house; it was during this time that he spotted Harry Norton. Tucker said he gestured to Harry from inside the house, asking for cigarettes, then went downstairs to retrieve the cigarettes and chatted a bit with Harry before he returned to the house. He denied walking up the street with Harry. A short time later Kris arrived at the house. Tucker stated that he went downstairs to let Kris in, and that after doing this they went upstairs to Tucker's bedroom to play video games and listen to music. We are then told that Kris told Tucker that he needed to "go out for a while" but "would be back soon."

Soon thereafter, Tucker testified, he saw Kris returning as promised. According to Tucker, Kris was walking down Rutland Street from the direction of Harkness Ave., which is in the opposite direction from the KC Market. Tucker testified that Kris stopped and talked a bit to a neighbor named Mike outside of the latter's house, which, again, is in the opposite direction from the KC Market. Mike stood out in that neighborhood because he owned a pink VW Beetle. Later in the trial, the lack of police follow-up to this reported conversation would be emphasized.

When Kris arrived back at Tucker's house, Tucker and Kris returned to the bedroom, but soon moved to the front room to look outside because they heard sirens. In a few minutes the doorbell rang, and they saw that it was the police. Tucker states that he then awakened his uncle, Stan Abrams, who had been sleeping after working the night shift. The three of them went down to the front gate where they were interviewed by SFPD officer William Brattan.

OFFICER WILLIAM BRATTAN

There is much more to mention about the testimony of Tucker Denton, but I now want to describe the findings of Officer Brattan, who very early responded to the 911 call and arrived at the store at around 9:20 A.M. He was immediately told by his superior to "case" the neighborhood. He did just that, knowing only that there had been a robbery and shooting. His first stop was at the house where Tucker lived.

The officer's first sight of Tucker was in response to his ringing the doorbell at around 9:35 A.M. Stan Abrams and Kris Davis soon followed Tucker to the front door and gate. Officer Brattan testified that Kris was "sweating bullets" while brushing his teeth. On cross examination we learn that this information was never included in the officer's police report. Officer Brattan did say that after asking their names and if any of them had heard anything in the neighborhood that morning, Kris responded that he "had heard three shots," and asked, "Is she going to be O.K.?" Tucker denied hearing any shots. Because of this inconsistency, and because Kris and Tucker were not in agreement when asked where Kris had slept the night before (Kris said he had slept at Tucker's house; Tucker said he'd slept at his own house) Brattan asked permission to enter the house and look around. Another officer accompanied Brattan and then they, Stan, Tucker and Kris went up into Tucker's bedroom, but they did not find much except for little evidence that Kris had slept there.

AT TUCKER'S HOUSE AFTER THE POLICE LEAVE THE FIRST TIME

One morning the judge compliments the jury for always being on time and for being understanding and patient. Two days later we must wait to start the proceedings because Ray, Juror #5, thought we were to start at a later time. We laughed because he is the son of a well-known judge, and he was the first to goof up. Ray also told us during a break the story about his visit years ago, along with his sister, to surprise their dad at work. They were both very young at the time. The bailiff let them into their father's chambers at the courthouse and the two children hid under Dad's desk to surprise him. They did not know that there was an emergency call buzzer hidden beneath the desk, and yes, they bumped into it. In rushed many police with guns drawn, only to find two surprised kids.

I realize that this story is becoming more and more convoluted, but these were the cards that we were dealt.

The next key scene at Tucker's house that day, April 3, includes Tucker, Kris Davis, and Dominique Lewis, whom we met earlier, albeit briefly. The time frame is after the robbery-murder, perhaps around 10:30 A.M., after Officer Brattan's visit. Tucker testified that Kris provided the three of them with a small bottle of Hennessy, which they shared while in the upstairs bedroom, and then pulled another from his pocket which somehow ended up in Tucker's dresser drawer and was found that afternoon by the police at the time of a formal search. Another Hennessy bottle was found on the stairway stuffed into a rolled-up carpet, and a third Hennessy bottle was discovered discarded near the curb across the street. The jury is shown photos of this evidence repeatedly throughout the trial.

At the trial both attorneys must work hard to get information from Tucker. We learn that early on April 3 he, too, was a KC Market customer (significance?), and that late in the morning 'he wandered down with others to Bayshore Boulevard, at least a mile away, to hang out at a 7-11 store. "I had a Slurpee. We were just chillin'."

Tucker then testified that later that day, while waiting for Kris at a bus stop near San Bruno Avenue, he noticed Kris pass by in a car driven by a friend known to both, namely Andrew Petty.

ANDREW PETTY'S FORD MUSTANG

Around 2:30 P.M. on April 3, Homicide Inspectors Cappelletti and Castro were notified

50 ml Hennessy cognac bottles
(Courtesy of Liquorverse.)

by Inspector Martin that a Ford Mustang had been discovered at the west end of Wilde Ave. This is a block away from the KC Market and relatively close to the home of Kris Davis. In it was evidence connected to the murder. To be specific, seven small Hennessy bottles; six in a green plastic garbage bag that was inside a blue backpack found on the front seat. The backpack also contained a bottle of gin and a bag of marijuana. There also was a Hennessy bottle beneath the driver's seat. Over and over again throughout the course of the trial the jury would be exposed to photos of the car and its contents.

Andrew Petty was the owner and driver of the car. Like most others in this story, he is well known to all within that neighborhood. He stated in his court testimony that in the early afternoon of April 3, he was driving past a Muni bus stop at the corner of San Bruno and Wilde Avenues when he saw some friends, including Kris Davis. According to Andrew, Kris had to be at work as a security patrolman at 3:00 P.M. Down the street from Kris's house and near a local school adjacent to McLaren Park they pulled over because "we had to pee."

We learned that Inspector Martin and his partner were scouting the neighborhood (in a light purple police car, no less) when they saw the Ford Mustang as it pulled up to park and "because it had a defective taillight." They apprehended both Andrew and Kris by drawing their guns and demanding that they get out of the car. Andrew and Kris obeyed. Kris, when asked, told the two policemen that the Hennessy bottles were his and that they were purchased in Oakland.

Kris responded affirmatively when asked if he was on parole. Andrew said the marijuana was his.

They were taken into custody separately and taken to adjacent, non-connecting rooms at the

Hall of Justice. At 5:20 P.M. Inspector Donovan, whom we will hear from later, performed a Gunshot Residue Test (GSR) on Kris Davis. None of the other witnesses in the trial were so tested. In the evening the Inspector then began a fingerprint analysis on all of the Hennessy bottles. More on the GSR later.

BULLETS

Sister Asale-Haquekyah was not part of the trial, but she caught my attention. It was during a lunch break and near the front steps at the Hall of Justice that I stopped to observe her. She was part of a group of about fifteen well-dressed black protesters who were rhythmically chanting and carrying signs that said that they were from THE PRESENT-DAY HEBREW NATION OF PEOPLES.

The noise from their hand-held battery-operated loudspeakers made it impossible to hear one another so she stepped away from the serpentine line that they had formed in order to talk to me one on one. I had not anticipated her doing this, so I was not sure what to say or ask, but "Tell me what this is all about" came out. They were protesting the fact that there are 150 unsolved homicides in San Francisco, with the majority of them being in their neighborhoods, and they were pleading for better police work to solve them. I wanted to tell her that I was a juror in such a murder case, but I didn't. I did wish her group success.

O.K., so at least three different sizes of Hennessy bottles were taken in the robbery- murder, and that same day three Hennessy bottles were found at the house where Tucker lived, and seven were found in the car occupied by Kris Davis and Andrew Petty. Now on to the bullets.

The jury was told by the San Francisco Medical Examiner that Mrs. Lee died of multiple gunshot wounds:

1. In and out of the left thigh.

2. Into the left thigh and through the left hip joint, with eventual lodging in her abdominal wall.

3. Through the left chest, aorta, liver and pancreas, ending in her lumbar area.

4. An in-and-out pathway starting in her left arm and out the same forearm.

The jury was shown photos taken in the morgue.

Inspectors Castro and Cappelletti were called by Mr. Lee the day after the murder because a bullet fragment was found on the floor of the KC Market. This was added to fragments removed from Mrs. Lee and sent to Mr. Terry Codman, who in 1999 was a ballistics expert employed by the SFPD. From him we heard about the general makeup and technology of bullets and that he can determine if a .38 caliber bullet was fired from a standard Colt revolver or from a semi-automatic gun. Because the bullets retrieved from Mrs. Lee and the one found on the market floor all had a "six-left twist" pattern when viewed under the microscope, Mr. Codman declared that all of these bullets were shot from the same gun and that the gun was not a semi-automatic.

MORE BULLETS

One morning when I arrived at juror seat #9 a cloud of dust appeared when I dropped my books and writing pad on the seat cushion. Alex, affectionately called Juror #8, saw this, and forcefully slapped his open hand on his seat cushion. A large dust imprint was the highly visible result. Judge Carson, who was standing nearby, noticed this and more or less apologized for the status of the entire courtroom. He then went on to say that courtroom renovations had been budgeted and approved for more than 18 months but that so far, nothing showed for it. I was sorry that he felt he had to comment upon a situation that had to be very frustrating to him.

At this point it is necessary to go back to the mid-afternoon of April 3, when both Andrew Petty and Kris Davis were apprehended because of the contents found in Andrew's Mustang.

Inspector Cappelletti was the main source of the next phase of this story with his account of the activities after the discoveries within the Mustang.

He wanted to do a search of Kris Davis's home but had to get permission. Not from Kris's mother, but from Kris's parole officer. This, apparently, is the law. Once obtained, the search was performed at the house, which was about halfway between the location of the parked Mustang and the KC Market. Mrs. Colville, Kris's mother, was present when the inspector found a small blue lockbox in a downstairs closet. After asking Mrs. Colville to open the box and calling the Hall of Justice to ask Kris to reveal the combination for the lockbox, Inspector Cappelletti forced the box open. Besides personal items such as pay stubs and some credit card information, there was a box of Remington .38 caliber bullets with 26 of the original 50 cartridges remaining. In a few days, Kris's fingerprints would be identified on the box and also on the actual carrier of the bullets. The blue box belonged to Kris.

Mr. Codman could not say that the bullets that killed Mrs. Lee were some of those that were missing from the box. But they were consistent.

James Breivis

AT THE HALL OF JUSTICE
THE EVENING OF APRIL 3, 1999

The Hall of Justice is a magnet for certain types of neighborhood commercial enterprises. Unique for me, certainly, are the nearly twenty bail bond establishments. During one lunch break I stopped into a few to look around, see if they had any printed literature and generally tried to learn something about this field of work. Most advertised that they covered all types of problems including sex crimes, burglary, narcotics, fraud and a host of others. I thought it ironic that they offered credit for services to people who might have committed a crime because they were out of money in the first place. Since they all pretty much offered the same services, I decided that if I ever needed bail, I would go to Dad's Bail Bonds, since I am a dad.

Inspector Donovan seemed to me to be a no-nonsense type of person; probably dull as hell, though, at a dinner party. As a crime scene investigator, he takes pictures of everything imaginable that is connected with a wrongdoing. He also identifies, bags and protects evidence, and is a fingerprint expert. Starting with the Mustang and its contents, he told us about his modus operandi for doing the above for the Hennessy bottles and the blue backpack with its other contents. The jury learned about the loops, whirls, and arches of fingerprints and the discipline of ACEV, or Analysis, Comparison, Evaluation and Verification.

From midafternoon into the late evening of April 3, he carefully did such work on the Lee murder case, initially on Wilde Avenue with the Mustang, and then later at the Hall of Justice. It was he who tested Kris Davis's hands for gunshot residue at around 5:25 P.M. Fingerprints he "lifted" from the Hennessy bottles in the car belonged to Kris Davis, Andrew Petty, and Tucker Denton. He did not find any prints of Mr. or Mrs. Lee on the ten Hennessy bottles.

It was much later that evening when Inspector Cappelletti interviewed Kris Davis and Andrew Petty separately at the Hall of Justice. The Inspector told the jury that Kris was wearing a 49er jacket and that in his possession were seven twenty-dollar bills. Nothing smaller in currency.

GSR

Robin, Juror #7, represents a rare phenomenon for a trial. She is an attorney, and they usually are excused from jury duty sometime during the selection process. A lot of her spare time during this trial was spent trying to do her work as the legal counsel for Mills College.

Steven Dowd was late for court. Something to do with a late plane arrival from Los Angeles, where he is a criminologist for the Los Angeles County Coroner's Office. As an expert witness for the prosecution, he was there to tell us all about gunshot residue. Dowd showed us a photo of a revolver exactly at the moment of firing a bullet. The photo also demonstrated the large "family of particles" emanating from the space near the cylinder as well as from the muzzle of the gun. This is true for all guns. These particles, consisting mainly of lead, barium, and antimony, land on and adhere to anything near the gun as it discharges. This includes hands, and according to Mr. Dowd, the particulate matter can be present for quite a while. They call it gunshot residue (GSR). The police rely on this occurrence in their investigations, and it is routine for them to do a GSR test on a suspect. Sticky tape is rolled over each hand, usually near the first web space, and the tape is then sent to experts like Mr. Dowd for analysis. As indicated above, the GSR sample was obtained from Kris Davis at around 5:25 P.M. on April 3, 1999, eight and a half hours after the murder of Mrs. Lee. From the microscopic analysis of the specimen from Kris Davis, two unique GSR particles were found on the right hand and several consistent (but not unique) on the left.

On cross examination of both Inspector Cappelletti and Mr. Dowd the jury learned that no other person involved in the Lee case was tested for GSR, that Kris's hands were never "bagged" when he was first apprehended, and that GSR, like dust particles anywhere, can be transferred from coincidental as well as specific contact with others. The defense attorney demonstrated the latter by showing that a cloth from a gun cleaning kit, when shaken near another person or even handled minimally by such a person who did not have prior contact with a gun, would distribute GSR onto this second individual. Also, two unique particles are far fewer than are usually seen from the hand sample of someone who recently fired a gun.

THE SAN QUENTIN TAPES

The clerk is someone who is in the middle of everything that occurs within the courtroom. Sophia Brennan, the clerk in Department 21, has been working there for over twenty years. The twelve of us stare at her every morning and afternoon and she stares back. Almost like each side looking through one-way mirrors at each other. She lives in Half Moon Bay, which is about 30 miles from work. Every day she bicycles to the courthouse from a location on Cesar Chavez Street, where she can park her car for free.

IMARS stands for Inmate Monitoring and Recording System and it is used to record each and every inmate phone call out of San Quentin. Only outgoing collect calls are allowed. Posted near every one of the 63 "public" phones at San Quentin is a sign saying that calls are recorded.

The jury heard the details of the technology of this system from the California Department of Corrections expert on it, Mr. Mike Peters. He seemed a bit nervous on the stand, dressed in his tightly buttoned blue blazer that looked like it was off the rack from Walmart.

The defendant, Kris Davis, was residing in that scenic complex by the San Francisco Bay in June 2002 when he made three collect phone calls out: two to his mother and a third to a girlfriend and his mother via a conference call. He was in prison due to a parole violation (presence of GSR and possession of ammunition) ascertained from the Lee murder case investigation.

For the sake of brevity, I have provided the reader with only excerpts from the taped telephone conversations between Kris Davis, his mother and a girlfriend, Michelle.

TAPE #1 (EXHIBIT 75A)

Mother: I got a subpoena to appear before the Grand Jury on this murder case.

Kris: Huh?

Mother: Yes, on the 20th of June.

Kris: Oh shit!

Mother: Yes.

Kris: Oh man.

Mother: They said this is the final stages of this, of this murder investigation. Well I don't know what these people expecting me to tell them except for what they (????), you remember that? That's the only thing I can see. I can't tell them jack shit.

Kris: Don't … when you go, don't say nothing.

Mother: You know, this is a grand jury. They do not fright.

Kris: You talk to Diane?

Mother: No, why I talk to that bitch for?

Kris: We got to … I got to find out what they talking about with Tucker. Man, do you know when you go to the grand jury … What I'm saying is, what they trying to do … when you go to this stuff … Now, I'm gonna try to call this man who, who had me subpoenaed and see what the hell this is all about. Alright Mama, I love you.

TAPE #2 (EXHIBIT 76A) THE SAME DAY

Kris: You can plead the 5th Amendment.

Mother: Oh, now you tell me how you know this.

Kris: Because I know somebody here that got down like that on the street. And they done been through it already. You could plead the 5th Amendment … they trying to bring forth all the evidence they have and to present it to … um … the jury … if it's enough evidence to indict me on the charge they give the DA permission to file charges on me … they trying to place me at the crime scene.

Mother: Well, they can't, because I talked to you. There's a "no win" situation. Now I don't know who they talking to, I don't know what kind of evidence they got, you know what I mean?

Kris: The grand jury, if they … if that grand jury find that I had anything to do with that, they supposed to come up here and get me and charge me with that. That's the whole point. If the … they gonna try to bring it all forth, all the evidence they got on … in a case, right? If the grand jury find anything in that case that they feel is enough evidence to bring me to court, they gonna get 'em to okay to arrest me on that case.

Mother: We know this. The point is ... there's nothing I can tell these people. I wasn't there. I wasn't in the neighborhood when this shit happened. There's nothing I can tell them. That's why I told you, those niggers down there wasn't your goddamn friends. Now I don't know what the hell has happened.

Kris: I'm wondering if they gonna call, I'm wondering if they gonna call Tucker as a witness?

Mother: A witness to what?

Kris: I don't know. He gave them a statement.

Mother: What statement did he give them?

Kris: When they ran up in the house. I don't know. That's the whole point, what they gonna try to do is, they gonna try to put me at the crime. If Tucker gave them a statement, they go ... they gonna subpoena him and try to make it whereas at the crime ... What ... if you don't find Diane then you ... and we don't know what Tucker gonna get up there and say. I could be going to jail.

Mother: First of all, they gotta prove it, that's number one.

Kris: No, that's the difference, Mama, the grand jury is different than the court. Why you think they taking the case to the grand jury? On the grand jury all they gotta do is present the case and if this ... if there's anything where the grand jury feels like I had something to do with it, they don't have to have solid evidence … what they gonna do is, they gonna ask you about the bullets that was found in the safe … all I know is Tucker told them that I was at Stan's.

Mother: And the only thing I can say is that you were here, 'cause I called here, and you answered the phone. I can't tell them what the suspect looked like, I can't tell them who was in the store, 'cause I was not there.

Kris: You know what you need to do? You need to call an attorney, right, and ask … ask the attorney … when you go to the grand jury, can you plead the 5th.

Mother: You damn right, I'm gonna plead something, 'cause I don't wanna get involved in …

Kris: All I know is, they got the bullets out the safe …

Mother: Huh?

Kris: They got the stuff that was in the safe. You know what I'm talking about? They got that; they got powder residue off my hand.

Mother: Powder residue?

Kris: Yeah … but he said all that is still not enough for them … for the jury to indict me … Yeah so, they gonna try to use somebody's statement to put me at the crime scene.

Mother: Listen … big back. You know when

I went to work?

Kris: Yeah.

Mother: And I called home ... and you answered the phone? And then Trina told me you was walking around in your underclothes?

Kris: I remember all that.

Mother: And remember I got mad at you?

Kris: But that's your statement, not mine ... your statement was I was at home, and you talked to me. My statement was I was at ... um ... Stan's house. (Note: Stan Abrams's, where Tucker lived, on Rutland St., near the store.)

Mother: Why did you say you was at Stan's house when you were at home?

Kris: I was at Stan's house. I had left the house after I talked to you and went to Stan's house.

Mother: Okay, but I bet the woman was already shot before that.

Kris: I don't know when. I don't know when ... I told them I was at Stan's house with Tucker ... Tucker told me that he told them that I was at his house with him.

Mother: Then there's nothing to lie about.

Kris: But I don't know, man, I'm still not taking no chances ... they gonna be trying to figure out, during the time that this happened, I was supposed to be at their house, did I ever go to the store? They trying to put me there. They trying to put both of us there, or one of us … if he talk and say the wrong thing, I'm getting indict …

Mother: Like I said, I told you this before since you was a little kid, you need to quit hanging with those niggers.

Kris: I already know that. If they indict me, that ain't the only thing I got to worry about.

Mother: What else you got to worry about?

Kris: The death penalty! When they was on the news, they said it was a hit, a hit robbery … they think she was telling something and that's why she got killed … but in the process of her getting killed they took something out the store … some alcohol … and if they subpoena Tucker, he gonna be there for about two or three hours … that boy dumb, there ain't no telling what he liable to say. That's who need to take the 5th, him …

TAPE #3 (EXHIBIT 77) FOUR DAYS LATER

Kris: You know, they subpoenaed Tiana?

Mother: For what?

Kris: 'Cause remember, they found those pictures and stuff in the house? 'Cause remember … um … I had told her to come to my hearing and tell 'em that the bullets were hers

… remember when they found the bullets in the house, Mama? And you remember, I was messing with her at the time. I had told her to come to the hearing and say the bullets was hers, so I wouldn't get the violation. But what they did was, when they went to her house, she wasn't there but her mom let them search her room and they found that letter … anyway, what else was I gonna ask you? Oh, I need you to call up her.

Mother: For what?

Kris: 'Cause they playing with my date. (Note: Release date from San Quentin.) I was supposed to come home on the 27th but they still talking about July 8th… what I'm saying is … I'd rather … be on the street … them trying to pick me up on the street than be in jail …

Mother: What's the difference?

Kris: A big difference. I got the chance to run, that's the big difference.

Mother: You not using your head. Think about what you say before you say it. We being recorded. If you run, you know two things are gonna happen to you. They gonna pick you up and beat the shit out of you, or either kill your ass, either or. And if you start running before you get off parole, you gonna do some more time.

Kris: I ain't that stupid.

END OF TAPES

So, there it is, edited by me, but for the most part as it was transcribed. The jury had copies of the transcriptions to review.

DOMINIQUE LEWIS

Compensation for jury duty in San Francisco is $15, plus $2.50 for transportation, per day, after the first day. Not sure why they even bother. Section 1.61.2 (a) of the IRS code states that "Jury duty is usually reported as taxable income on line 21 of form 1040." It just doesn't seem right.

The judge gave the jury the afternoon off the first time Dominique was scheduled to appear in court. He was incarcerated somewhere in central California and supposedly was being transported in, but they couldn't locate him. I thought this was humorous. Could not find the convict.

He was there the next morning, dressed in orange, surly, and looking either mean or dumb or both, I wasn't sure. There was no question that he was in the thick of street life around the Wilde/Rutland neighborhood and that he hung out with the defendant. Earlier we had heard that soon after the robbery-murder he was upstairs at Tucker's house sharing Hennessy with Tucker and Kris. In testimony given later by Inspector Castro we learned that Dominique was arrested on April 4, 1999, but we never heard for what.

Dominique's initial testimony, or lack of it, caught all of our attention. With his attorney by his side, his responses to questions from the prosecution were consistent: "For personal reasons I refuse to answer." The judge ordered him to answer, and he refused. Contempt of court was declared after each refusal. For some weird reason I thought of a parent ordering their kid to eat such and such at the dinner table and the kid saying "No." Just like a scene in a movie.

The judge ordered the jury out of the courtroom until further notice.

About 45 minutes later we reconvened, and Dominique apologized to the court (apology accepted) and announced that he would testify. He did. Well, sort of. He said he was like a big brother to Tucker Denton and that he looked out for him. To all other questions, with topics such as the Hennessy, the blue backpack, who he was with that day, etc., the answer was either "I can't recall" or "I'm not sure." So much for his testimony.

SKIN COLOR, JACKET DESCRIPTION, BAGS

While we were still hearing testimony, the well-covered Scott Peterson murder trial was concluding, about thirty miles south of San Francisco. What contrasts! Their public gallery was always filled to capacity, the press coverage was enormous and every day, updates and guessing games were a regular feature of the media. Our trial, which also involved a horrible murder, seldom attracted any observers and no press. Such is death.

Whoever murdered Mrs. Lee was black and was wearing a jacket. The ski mask and gloves made further skin identification difficult. In a police interview performed on April 9, 1999, Mr. Lee said that the robber had "very black skin" based on what he observed on the neck. Later on, he was not so sure.

Another witness named Amin, who will be further mentioned soon, said the fleeing robber's skin color was "olive." Kris Davis is a light-skinned black man.

Both Amin and Mr. Lee initially told the police that the robber was wearing a green jacket. Actually, Mr. Lee said the torso was green and the sleeves either beige or yellow. In November 2002, at a follow-up police interview, Amin remembered that the jacket had white sleeves.

Tucker owned a green jacket. Inspector Cappelletti took it and showed it to Mr. Lee, who said, "No, that wasn't it."

Many, many people stated that Kris Davis constantly wore a 49er jacket that was red with some black in it. Certainly, no green.

A full-length photo taken when Kris was taken into custody has him staring at us, head tilted a bit, wearing his 49er jacket. Just one of the 49er faithful!

Earlier on I mentioned that the police found a blue backpack in the front seat of the Mustang within which there was a dark green garbage bag containing Hennessy bottles. Nowhere else was a blue backpack mentioned in connection with the crime. Mr. Lee told the police on April 9, 1999, that he thought the bag used in the store robbery was a brown sports bag. Amin said the robber was carrying a bag but could not recall the color.

HEIGHT, WEIGHT, BUILD OF ROBBER-MURDERER

As a juror I found keeping trial information to myself to be very difficult. It seemed so contrary to human nature. I wanted to discuss the various aspects of the testimony I heard every day since it was so interesting and complex. I know my fellow jurors felt the same way.

Three people saw the murderer. One is dead. The other two are Mr. Lee and Amin Ahmad.

Mr. Lee testified that the man was tall and was of "average weight." Attempts to obtain more specifics were unsuccessful.

AMIN AHMAD

He would be one of only two witnesses called by the defense. At the time of the trial, he was an airline pilot, married and living far from the Harkness Avenue home in which he was living in April of 1999. On the witness stand he was a well-dressed, thin, nervous young man with Arabic features who responded to questions using a low voice.

Harkness and Wilde Avenues run parallel to each other and are connected by Rutland Street, which actually is quite short.

Mr. and Mrs. Lee purchased the KC Market, on the corner of Wilde Ave. and Rutland St., from Amin's father six months before the shooting. Amin testified that he knew Kris Davis, the defendant, back in 1999 because Kris would frequently come into the store for purchases. When not in school, Amin sometimes worked in the store. Mr. Addison, the defense attorney, carefully extracted the story about Amin's experiences relating to the robbery and murder.

Somewhere around 8:00 A.M. on April 3, 1999, Amin left his house, which was about a block from the KC Market. He walked east on Harkness Ave., turned south onto Rutland, and after walking about two-thirds of the distance toward the store he stopped when he heard at least two gunshots. The shots preceded the noise of the store's front door motion buzzer going on and off.

The next few moments were very frightening for him because he described to us his seeing a man wearing a dark ski mask with two eye holes running out of the store with gun in hand.

He cannot recall one way or the other if the man was carrying a bag. As the robber diagonally crossed Rutland and proceeded up the opposite side of the street from where Amin was now crouching behind a parked car, eye contact was made. Amin later told the police that the man wore a green jacket, was husky, and about six feet two inches tall. Amin told the jury that this was a dangerous neighborhood, and he knew that he had just witnessed a robber pass closely in front of him while fleeing the store. He was very concerned about his own safety.

We are told by Amin that he waited behind the parked car until he saw the robber run up

Rutland St. and get into a white van near the corner of Harkness Ave. and Rutland St.

Amin then went to the front door of the KC Market, looked in, and saw Mr. Lee screaming while holding his wife. The telephone next to them was dangling off the hook. When asked, Mr. Lee told Amin that yes, he had called 911. Sirens in the neighborhood were getting louder.

Amin then testified that police were on the scene very fast and that he told a police officer who was outside the store that he had seen the robber escape up the street. He pointed towards Harkness Ave., told the officer about the white van, and gave the officer a note with his name and phone number on it for their investigation. He told us that he quickly left the area of the crime. Later that afternoon he spotted the white van near the same corner, namely Harkness Avenue and Rutland Street. He told us that he phoned the police with this information and supplied them with a partial license plate number.

"Was the robber wearing gloves?" the defense attorney asked.

"I can't recall," Amin responded.

From other defense questions we learn that early on after the incident, Amin told the police that the escaping robber did not look like Kris. "The robber was more big-boned than Kris

Davis," he said.

At the police station, soon after the crime, Amin was shown mug shots of many men, including the characters covered in this story. Positive identification never occurred. The defense attorney specifically asked Amin if he believed he saw Kris Davis outside the store at any time on April 3, 1999. Amin said "No."

Forty-three months after the shooting, on Thanksgiving of 2002, the San Francisco police came unannounced to Amin Ahmad's house for questioning. He was now married, living elsewhere, and employed as an airline pilot. On that November day he was at work; his wife, we are told, was frightened by the police. He subsequently made an appointment to come in for questioning and we learned that at this later date his descriptions of the jacket of the robber (maybe light-colored sleeves) and what else the robber might have been carrying (maybe there was a light bag in the right hand) conflicted with his earlier version.

Amin told the jury that it was only three months before this trial that he heard, much to his surprise, that Kris Davis had been arrested and charged with the murder of Mrs. Lee.

The jury never heard anything more about the white van. Specifics about its existence, any follow-up by the police or any other information never surfaced.

JACK LANE

Mr. Lane lived at the junction of Harkness Avenue and Rutland Street. From his driveway one can look down Rutland and see the awning of the store. On the day of the crime police interviewed him, and notes of that conversation revealed that Mr. Lane was outside working on his truck when he heard some shots, looked up, and saw two darkly-dressed men with hoods leaving the store and turning up Wilde Ave.

On the witness stand at the trial Mr. Lane could not remember anything. My guess was he had Alzheimer's disease.

JUROR INSTRUCTIONS

Judge Carson was extremely thorough and meticulous with protocol and information throughout the trial. In general, he told us, there would be three parts to his final instructions:

1. General principles of evidence.
2. Definition of crimes.
3. Our duties and conduct as jurors.

GENERAL PRINCIPLES

We must apply the law to facts that have been proven by the evidence. Facts can be proved by both direct and circumstantial evidence. Factors include how aware any witness is and how biased the witness might be.

THE CRIMES

The defendant, Kris Davis, is charged with first degree murder including special circumstances. Only if we find him not guilty of that offense are we to consider a verdict of murder in the second degree. In addition, there are two counts of robbery.

THE CONDUCT AND DUTIES OF THE JURY

We are to deliberate as a group and yet make individual assessments and decisions. Do not tolerate nor give undue influence. The foreman of the jury will upon completion of the verdict write out results on the forms provided by the court. The jury may request that any court testimony be read back to them.

Included in the written jury instructions was a definition of reasonable doubt. This definition had been read to prospective jurors a month earlier and we, the final jurors, would refer to it frequently during our deliberations. Reasonable doubt is not a mere possible doubt, because everything relating to human affairs is open to some possible or imaginary doubt. Reasonable doubt is that state of the case which, after the entire comparison and consideration of all the evidence, leaves the minds of the jurors in the condition that they cannot say they feel an abiding conviction of the truth of the charge. The burden is on the prosecution to prove beyond a reasonable doubt that the defendant is the person who committed the crime or crimes charged.

If after considering the circumstances of the identification and any other evidence in this case you have a reasonable doubt whether the defendant was the person who committed the crime, you must give the defendant the benefit of that doubt and find him not guilty.

CLOSING STATEMENTS BY THE PROSECUTION

Mr. Hallinan told us that it was his burden and responsibility to present us with the evidence that Mrs. Lee's murder was premeditated and deliberate, and that it was committed by Kris Davis. Now it was up to us to come to that conclusion and find him guilty of first-degree murder including special circumstances. On a screen he showed a slide whose heading said "Evidence of Guilt" and below it were three words: time, place, and manner. He reminded us that early on the morning of April 3, Kris called Tucker Denton to say, "I'm coming over." When he separated from Tucker, it was during this segment of time, at approximately 9:10 A.M., that he committed the crime.

Officer Brattan arrived at the threshold of Tucker's house at 9:35 A.M. In response to his ringing, he told the jury that Kris, along with Tucker and Stan Abrams, came to the front gate. "Kris Davis was sweating bullets and brushing his teeth." When asked, Tucker said he had not heard any shots; Kris's response to the question was, "I heard three shots. Is she going to be O.K.?"

Hennessy bottles were found not only at Tucker's house, where we are told that they first appeared out of Kris's pockets soon after the shooting, but also that seven – "yes, seven" – were found in the Mustang in which Kris Davis was a passenger. Kris's fingerprints were identified on some of the bottles.

Mr. Hallinan emphasized that he did not think we should believe that the cognac bottles were a coincidental finding.

As to the three separate instances in which Ricardo Nevins was consistent in his recollection of encountering Kris in front of the store with a gun in his waistband and the words, "I'm gonna do her," Mr. Hallinan emphasized that only when Ricardo had to face Kris in court did he call his earlier three testimonies a lie.

Another slide shown by the prosecutor listed the scientific evidence in the case that was never refuted by the defense. They are the cause of death, fingerprint analysis, ballistics and bullet analysis and finally, the GSR analysis.

The recorded phone conversations in 2002 of Kris Davis from San Quentin are not, according to Mr. Hallinan, the words of an innocent man. Specifically, he cited Kris's insistence that Tucker be located before he ever appeared before the grand jury, that his mother plead the 5th Amendment when testifying, and that "we need to get our stories straight."

CLOSING STATEMENTS
BY THE DEFENSE

Before documenting the final statements of Mr. Floyd Addison, the public defender, I need to state how very impressed I was with the professional conduct and competence of both opposing attorneys as well as the judge. By this point in the trial, I had seen them in action for over five weeks. I also sensed a respect for one another between them.

Frequently during the many days of testimony, we would be exposed to convincing responses from a witness and in the back of my mind I would ask, "I wonder how the other side is going to deal with that piece of information, or that bit of evidence, etc." More often than not, the other side would impress me with their methodologies. They were professionals. After the closing statements of the prosecution, I was anxious to hear the counterpoints of the defense.

Mr. Addison started by telling us he really was not sure exactly what he would end up saying to us, on this his last occasion to influence us to find the defendant not guilty.

He started by saying not guilty is very different than being innocent. Kris Davis was not innocent, by any means. "We all know that."

The overhead slide that he had on the screen asked, "Do we have a doubt?" He then showed us a poster board blowup of the words that defined reasonable doubt.

He went on to describe the cultural attitude of the people toward the police in the Wilde/Rutland section of Visitacion Valley. He said that all black men are looked upon as suspects for any crime, are stopped and questioned with little reason, and thus, of course, they view the police differently than, say, you or me. This sometimes leads to lying.

Mr. Addison repeated what he had said in his opening statement of the trial, namely, that the police lasered in on Kris Davis and overlooked other suspects and procedures because they were not open-minded in their pursuit to solve the crime. He described it as an unconscious bias. He gave examples. Why was Kris Davis the only person tested for GSR? Why not Andrew Petty, who was driving the Mustang? And the police seemed to overlook protocol as well as leads. He said the police even admitted that the hands of both Kris Davis and Andrew Petty should have been bagged. Why did the police never seek follow-up information on the white van seen and partially identified by Amin? And how about finding out if the neighbor Mike actually did see and talk to Kris Davis on Rutland St. during those critical minutes around the time of the murder?

We are told that the jury heard direct evidence from four individuals. Everything else is circumstantial. The four are Mr. Lee, Ricardo Nevins, Jack Lane and Amin Ahmad. Neither Mr. Lee nor Amin could positively identify the murderer as being Kris Davis. Skin color, jacket color, body build, and height are all described differently at different times, even by the same witnesses. Neighbor Jack Lane cannot help us now with any recollection. He has none.

Mr. Addison then asked us to consider the scene and later photos around the apprehension of Kris Davis and Andrew Petty. Looking at the jury he put forth the question, "In your neighborhood is it common practice for the police to check on defective taillights by having their guns drawn and demanding that the occupants come out with their hands up? The photo of the blue bag on the front seat of the Mustang with the liquor bottle hanging out and the marijuana bag exposed and the garbage bag sticking out – doesn't that photo seem a little staged to you?" he asked. "Doesn't it seem strange that all these items are sitting there perfectly exposed for the photographer?"

As for everything else, such as the bullets, the bottles, the GSR, and the prints, "They are circumstantial and not direct evidence."

FINAL COMMENTS BY THE PROSECUTION

The judge informed us that the prosecution had the final opportunity to speak but could only use the time to refute comments made by the defense in their closing statement.

I mentioned earlier my trying to anticipate retorts or responses of one attorney to another. I was very surprised by the tactic used at this final opportunity by Mr. Hallinan.

He chose to ridicule the thought process of his opponent, particularly any possible bias by the police, and especially the thought of staging something like the initial appearance of the blue backpack in the Mustang. Mr. Hallinan then ranted and raged that Mr. Addison then must believe that the police planted the bullets, and that the police must have had Hennessy bottles in their cars and placed them at Tucker's house and in the Mustang. He went on in such a way for quite a while and then something occurred that truly surprised me.

Mr. Hallinan told us to imagine explaining this trial to a friend at a later date and after describing the evidence how any third party could possibly come up with a verdict other than guilty. And then Mr. Hallinan's facial muscles quivered, his voice broke, and tears flowed down his cheeks after saying that we, the jury, owed Mr. Lee a guilty verdict in the name of Justice. Mr. Hallinan then went to the prosecution table, sat down and wept.

THE BALL IS IN OUR COURT

The deliberation room for the jury hadn't seen a housekeeper for a very long time and the ambiance was horrific. Our chairs were of three varieties, and few seemed to originally be intended to be there. Somewhere on the other side of the walls, but close by, were doors that were frequently slammed with a vengeance.

The bailiff went over the rules. We had to stop discussing the case whenever he came into the room. If we needed him there was a buzzer to push on one of the walls. Within the confines of the area were two restrooms. The cart carrying the items officially entered as evidence was rolled in, and he then locked the door. The transition from our passive to active state had occurred very quickly.

Someone spoke up and asked if anyone wanted to volunteer to be the foreman. I said I would do it if the group wished, and that was that. I had anticipated something like this based on some comments made by other jurors earlier during breaks. I had always enjoyed group processes and felt comfortable in this role.

We weren't in that room for more than five minutes when we found it necessary to ring the bailiff. Nobody had arranged to supply us with blackboard chalk, and we needed more poster board paper.

I saw everyone staring at me for a beginning. I told them I appreciated their confidence and that my intention was not necessarily to lead, but to guide. I told them that I had some suggestions for both the philosophy and conduct of the forthcoming process, and that I would now state them. Once I was finished, I would open this initial discussion to the other eleven. I stated that we were all one-twelfth of a talented decision-making group with a tough task ahead, and that I hoped each juror would show respect for the opinions of each other.

1. Please allow whoever is speaking to finish. Only one speaker is to talk at a time. If you agree, if you have something to say while another juror is speaking, raise your hand and I will make sure that you will be heard.

2. We would have work lunches with short breaks in order to move along.

3. Since it was December 21, this deliberation could possibly go beyond Christmas. Many jurors had travel plans for the holidays that would have to change should we not finish by the end of December 23.

4. As hard as this might be on one's personal life, we owed it to the Lee family, the

defendant, and all others to do this thing correctly. I asked that they accept the possibility of a long deliberation.

There were no objections or alternatives offered to my suggestions. I then stated that in my opinion we would not have to decide individual verdicts (first- or second-degree murder, two counts of robbery) concerning Kris Davis. Our decision should be a collective one, meaning that he and he alone was either guilty of first-degree murder plus the robbery, or he was not guilty.

The jurors readily agreed.

I had read somewhere that other juries had often begun with a non-binding straw vote. When two from our group opposed this for a variety of reasons, including a wish to go over the evidence, I said "no vote now" and asked for opinions on how we should proceed. The two choices offered were documenting a timeline of the known events of April 3, 1999, or going over some of the evidence such as the Hennessy bottles, the bullets, the GSR, etc.

The timeline suggestion was the unanimous choice. One of the jurors offered to do the charting and so we were on a roll.

For the next thirty minutes the blackboard slowly gained notations such as 9:17 A.M. for the 911 call, 9:35 A.M. for the time Officer

Brattan first stopped at Tucker's house, etc.

Suddenly and without warning a juror spoke up and declared how disgusted he was with the final statements of the prosecutor, Mr. Hallinan. Four or five others echoed the sentiment. I too had a negative reaction to it, but I wanted to get the jurors back on track with the timeline.

Actually, they did too, and the venting over that final tactic of the prosecutor served its purpose. It never again was a topic of discussion.

It had been an exhausting day for all of us and the 4:30 closing time arrived. Everyone wanted to resume at 9:00 A.M. the next morning, but one juror said he just could not handle it that early. I did not force the issue. I said, "Tomorrow at 9:30 and please, nobody gets sick." Prior to us actually leaving, the judge had to reconvene the court in order to have the recess documented, along with the usual admonition to us to not discuss anything until we reassembled.

DECEMBER 22

Our jury of nine men and three women included one Black and one Filipino. With all the interruptions for courtroom breaks, for lunch and by order of the judge, we'd had a lot of opportunities over the past four weeks to chat and get to know one another. Or did we really? On my way to court that day I felt that we would have a vote sometime that morning. So far, I believed each of the other eleven was a levelheaded, intelligent person and I liked them all. But then again, we hadn't been challenged at all regarding how well we absorbed the evidence, digested it, regurgitated it in the cramped deliberation room and rendered an opinion. Were any of the others extremists? How about racists, or severe law and order advocates? Would there be outbursts? I knew that this day would be eventful. I personally intended to listen closely to the discussions because I was on the fence regarding my vote.

The judge that day had somehow found funding for us to have our ordered lunches paid for by the City and County of San Francisco. We had previously been told this was no longer the case because of the budget crunch. So, when we were reassembled in the room, we did not resume discussing the timeline of April 3, 1999; we individually ordered our lunches! The bailiff took the twelve sheets of orders and locked the door.

The group agreed to refine the timeline information and was doing an admirable job of it when in the space of ten minutes two things happened. Juror #7 tapped me on the shoulder and said he had to lie down because he was ill.

I asked if he felt he could still participate, and he nodded in the affirmative. So there he was, lying on the floor with a seat cushion for a pillow. While I was informing the others about our ill colleague, keys could be heard rattling in the door. The bailiff walked in, and of course we all became silent. He unfolded a paper that I thought was a note to us from the judge. I was wrong. He calmly said that Juror #1 did not indicate what condiments he wanted on his sandwich! I couldn't believe what I was witnessing. I had always thought that there was sanctity or something similar in this deliberation process. Mayonnaise was checked off.

In our timeline discussion we agreed that Kris's mother probably did call home from work on the morning of April 3, 1999, but that she was wrong on the time. It had to have been earlier than 9:15. The cigarette exchange between Tucker and Harry Norton had to have occurred before Kris first came over to Tucker's house. Then the statements of Ricardo Nevins with respect to the 10:00 A.M. time that he had seen Kris in front of the store (with the gun, "I'm gonna do her") had to be way off. In fact, we diverged from the timeline to discuss Ricardo.

We knew that some of the testimony of Ricardo, Tucker, Andrew, Dominique and others contained lies. On the stand two of them even admitted it. How on earth were we supposed to stratify or "prioritize" lies? What we decided to do was to chart a so-called individual juror option list to choose from when deciding on where one stood on Ricardo Nevins's testimonies. Choice one was that he was truthful the first three times he was interviewed and lied on the stand; choice three was that he lied throughout; in between was the possibility that he did indeed see Kris in front of the store before Mrs. Lee was shot but that there never was an exposed gun nor that statement from Kris. These choices were posted.

It was around 10:15 and the jurors needed a break. I buzzed for the bailiff and learned that in order for us to leave the room and stretch and satisfy our bladders the judge would reconvene the court just to announce the ten-minute interruption. Damn protocol. We could have stayed within these confines, but there were two smokers amongst us. During our break Juror #7 called me aside and stated he was too ill to continue. He was perspiring and seemed to have a fever. When the judge reconvened to announce that we would resume deliberating I asked to approach the bench. I told him that Juror #7 had a problem, so he announced that he would talk to me "in chambers" and sent the other eleven back to the room with orders to wait.

I had wondered what things looked like behind the courtroom. The answer was cage-like partitions similar to a large kennel. In here some Homo sapiens were within the cages.

Upon entering the judge's chamber, he greeted me with questions about my career as a physician and then proceeded to tell me about his prior experience with his own back pain and sciatica, what was done by his treating orthopedic surgeon, how well he was doing, etc. I listened for a while and then I informed him of the sick juror. He had me repeat this information with the court reporter present and then interviewed Juror #7 himself while I spent the next hour waiting for the outcome with the other jurors. Of course this extended into lunchtime. Outside it was raining, but the black cloud seemed to be within the building and suspended over the jurors from Diepartment 21. The judge then announced that we were excused until the afternoon, when the alternate juror was expected to arrive. We all knew that the rules state that should an alternate be activated, deliberations must start from scratch.

I erased the blackboard and removed the poster papers. Photographs of the KC Market and the map of the neighborhood stayed pinned to the walls. The group didn't gripe, and they were eager to proceed.

What a surprise when I asked for suggestions on how to restart and someone raised their hand and offered to initiate a day-of-the-crime timeline. With precision the jurors all contributed to a (new) timeline and our conclusion was that Kris Davis could have committed the crime. Nothing from the time analysis ruled him out. Now this wasn't particularly an earthshaking discovery, but it arrived in an analytical manner via a group process. To me it signified a move forward after a very frustrating day so far.

A juror then announced that he believed a discussion centering on the Hennessy bottles was a critical next step. Nobody had a particularly strong alternative topic, so the happenings at Tucker's house, with emphasis on the Hennessy bottles, were rehashed. It seemed likely that Kris was the source of the Hennessy bottles shared with Tucker and Dominique in the morning right after the murder. But then again, our sources for this information were Tucker and Dominique, and we knew that they had lied in other areas of questioning. The finding of more Hennessy bottles in the Mustang that same day certainly implicated Kris. But did the fact that he had a connection to ten Hennessy bottles mean that he pulled the trigger? Was there evidence to lead us to that conclusion? It was an open question that was left unanswered.

With help from the group, a juror stood and charted other topics for possible discussion. They included bullets, GSR, Amin, police M.O. (modus operandi), prison tapes, fingerprints, jacket(s), motive, and behavior of Kris on the day of the murder.

Another suggestion was to proceed with an examination of the sources of the direct evidence that the defense attorney, Mr. Addison, had listed in his closing statement to us, the jury. There were four in number. Mr. Lee, Ricardo Nevins, Jack Lane, and Amin Ahmad.

Ricardo Nevins was already discussed. Jack Lane, we eliminated as a worthwhile or workable source since his original statements were in conflict with other, more likely testimony and he no longer had a memory. Perhaps he was losing his memory back in 1999. That left Mr. Lee and Amin.

The discussion around Mr. Lee and his testimony went on for at least an hour and led to a jury agreement on the following: that he had confirmed, and was the source of, the tale of the robbery-murder, the Hennessy bottles, earlier or pre-murder store customers, the phone call by the arrested hijacker to Mrs. Lee, and the visit to the store by the friend of the hijacker. However, his description of the robber-murderer neither ruled out Kris Davis as the one who did it, nor ruled him in.

A juror then raised his hand and stated that the testimony of Amin Ahmad was unreliable. Others felt differently. As we were closing for the day another juror asked if we could ask the judge for a reading back of the testimony of Mr. Ahmad. My request for this to the judge was granted and would occur first thing the next morning.

This day had seen a series of delays, mainly due to the need to get a substitute for the sick juror. We were exhausted, discouraged and in recess. Outside, people were bustling about with their Christmas shopping. I felt frazzled and walked part of the way home. I kept thinking about tomorrow and my vote.

DECEMBER 23 – WILL WE ARRIVE AT A VERDICT?

It was around 3:00 A.M. when I awoke thinking about gunshot residue and Hennessy bottles. To pass the time I checked my e-mail, did some laundry, and tried to read. Preoccupied would be putting it mildly. By the time I left for court I had mistakenly washed my wallet with my other items, put that day's newspaper into the recycling bin and forgotten to take my morning medicine. And I thought about the jurors who had made plans to fly out that evening, some for extended periods. I decided to ask the jurors if they wanted me to approach the judge and see if he would write letters to the airlines for flight refunds. Also, if we were to extend our deliberations beyond Christmas, maybe he would allow an extra day off before we reconvened.

It turned out that none of this was necessary. Every juror, when asked, said that they had rearranged their schedules and that a December 27 return, if needed, would be fine. There was no bitching or moaning. "Let's get started."

The court reporter brought the typewritten testimony of Amin Ahmad into the deliberation room.

As she read it, we all had in front of us the courtroom-issued notebooks with our own notations of his testimony of three days previously. She left when she finished, and as we started to deliberate again, in came the bailiff. This time somebody didn't indicate what type of bread they wanted for their sandwich. For some reason the interruption didn't bother me so much this time.

An interesting thing occurred when the stopping of the Mustang by the police came up. Many of us thought the police excuse of a faulty taillight was "a stretch." The newest juror pointed out the photograph with the red tape covering the taillight area. All of us had stared at that photograph at least ten times during the trial and few had noticed the tape job. I was one who hadn't.

The group decided to talk more about the Hennessy bottles, the fingerprints, the bullets and the GSR. Collectively we accepted the scientific aspects such as the testimonies of the experts, the application of the technology, and the handling of the specimens. What it seemed to come down to was how much weight each of us would give to all of this circumstantial information in our verdict. We decided to have our lunch and then have our first vote.

Since the court did not even supply paper for the balloting, I stole some type of court schedule sheets from the clerk's desk and on the blank side wrote "guilty" with a blank block next to those words, and in a similar pattern "not guilty" below. Immediately after lunch, ballots were distributed and quickly returned. I opened the folded papers and read the votes. Eight guilty and four not guilty.

This was the first time since we were sworn in that we were no longer an amorphous body, but a group divided. I was worried that this polarization would develop into dysfunctional behavior. And where should we go from here?

We chose to locate the definition of reasonable doubt and it was read aloud. Then a few volunteered to speak up about how they had voted and why. I revealed that my not guilty opinion was based on reasonable doubt despite the accumulated circumstantial evidence stacked up against the defendant. Yes, he was a "scum bag" and certainly not innocent, but I had difficulty sending him to prison for a very long time based on the indirect evidence. Some agreed. Others didn't.

To some, the accumulated evidence of Hennessy bottles, the statement of Kris Davis to Officer Brattan around 9:35 A.M. on April 3, the GSR, the bullets and the Ricardo Nevins testimony was enough to consider Kris guilty. "A slam dunk," one juror said.

What didn't happen amongst the jurors at this point was more important to me than what did happen. Friends of mine who had served on other juries had related to me their experience with anger, insults, and rudeness at such a juncture. This never occurred with this group, and I am not exactly sure why not, because a lot of thought and "ownership" had gone into each juror's decision. I read acceptance in many expressions around the table. However, I was unable to interpret and expand on acceptance. At least to me, the other eleven did not seem too surprised by the outcome of the first ballot.

For a while the jury was treading water. A woman juror (with the substitution there were now four women jurors) said she wanted to review her notes. Good idea. As foreman, I recommended that the group stay in the room, keep chatter to a minimum, review their notes or evidence or just meditate, and we would begin group discussions in fifteen to twenty minutes. I detected relief on many faces.

During the silent period I closed my eyes and hoped for some clairvoyance. Actually, a new issue did pop up. We had never once heard about a motive for Kris Davis to commit such a crime. Only through speculation could one be created. For me, this provided some type of deep, internal reassurance regarding my "not guilty" persuasion. But was I creating something like an excuse to stick to my opinion, or did I really have reasonable doubt?

When we reconvened, there was some discussion around the failure of the police to bag some hands to preserve GSR, to check with neighbor Mike on Rutland, or to pursue the white van lead. But we had to deal with the evidence provided in court.

The jurors more or less voted for me to inform the judge that we were deadlocked. I told them that we could do this only after another vote because the judge would never accept this outcome after only a single vote. Again, there were no disagreements, thank God. When the ballots were counted it was now six and six. I wrote a note to the judge.

It was about forty-five minutes before the principals were assembled for the judge to reconvene the proceedings. He read my note to the court. "We are hung." He requested more information and as foreman I was the one who responded. "How many times did the jury vote, and when did this take place?" the judge asked. While responding I thought to myself, "I sure am glad I insisted on that second vote."

"And without indicating exactly how the vote went, tell me the numbers." I told him eight and four the first time and six and six the second.

The judge, after conferring with both attorneys, told us to quit for the day, go home, have a great holiday, and return on December 27 to continue with the jury deliberations. And, he added, "Perhaps it would be best to not even think about this trial over the long weekend."

As we all left the court and headed for the front door, "Merry Christmas" was heard repeatedly, along with "See you Monday."

MONDAY, DECEMBER 27

We were getting better because the first stab at selecting a choice for lunch went without incident. Earlier the bailiff showed us the deep blue water goblets that he had won in the office Christmas drawing. I just cannot picture him ever using them, but who knows.

I entered the deliberations that day without any predetermined action plan or strategy. My hope that someone else had over the weekend come up with an "Aha" and an idea on how we might move along didn't materialize either. And yet, here we were with the assignment of trying to reach a unanimous verdict.

"How about someone who voted guilty elaborate on their reasons, and then the opposite. Perhaps that will influence our thoughts." This suggestion came from a person who I thought had previously switched opinions, but it did not receive much support because, as one juror said, "Haven't we done that already?"

A decision was made to listen again to the taped conversations of Kris Davis's three 2002 phone calls to his mother when Kris was in San Quentin. It seemed to me that the same issue arose here as with the other circumstantial evidence. Collectively, all of it convinced some jurors that Kris was either very unlucky or guilty of first degree murder and they thought, in the end, the latter.

Lunchtime came quickly and went. In the afternoon we were repeating ourselves and knew it. I asked every person to tell me if they believed that as individuals and as a group, had we done our best? Next, does anyone believe more deliberating would help? Yes and no were the answers.

We took another vote, and it was seven to five, with the seven voting guilty. This time my note to the judge was longer, but with the same bottom line.

The judge asked me, and then each juror, the same questions that were posed earlier in the deliberation room. A mistrial was declared. The judge delivered a lengthy speech thanking us all and terminated the trial.

Kris Davis looked relieved but there were no cheers, no tears, and no hanging around. The jurors gathered around the attorneys and asked questions that will be covered in the epilogue.

Who shot Suzie Q? Yes, it could have been Kris Davis. But then again, I'm not sure.

EPILOGUE

The District Attorney's office in 1999 twice turned down the opportunity to proceed with the Lee murder prosecution, apparently because of the lack of enough evidence (source: Counsel Hallinan). Then in 2002 the law was changed to allow taped phone conversations into court.

Mr. Hallinan, the prosecutor who was assigned to this case in 2001, told me that he spent over 50 days at San Quentin in 2002 in order to obtain the taped phone conversations between Kris Davis and his mother.

Our trial was the second mistrial. In September 2004 the first mistrial was called after jury selection, opening arguments, and some testimony, when the information from Mr. Lee about his wife commenting about a "pitiful person" appeared for the very first time. The defense objected because they had not been informed about it beforehand. The judge sustained the objection and declared a mistrial.

Despite the high crime rate in the area, neighbors and friends were shocked and outraged over the murder at the store. Mr. and Mrs. Lee had lived above the store and had brought to that small segment of the neighborhood a significant infusion of optimism and accomplishment with the introduction of fresh vegetables and other marked improvements to a corner store that previously had been known to sell primarily liquor and tobacco. Children posted "We will miss you Suki" signs on the store windows, and fresh cut flowers were on the doorstep for weeks.

Mr. Addison stated that unless there is a very, very good reason for the defendant to testify, he discourages it. And with a reported I.Q. of 77, Kris Davis would have been mincemeat on the witness stand for the prosecutor.

At the trial the jury was fed minimal information about the carjacking. In a San Francisco Examiner article covering the crime, I learned that this perpetrator, too, wielded a gun and was wearing a ski mask. This was confirmed as well as the fact that Clint Britten, the man arrested for the hijacking, knew the victim and insisted that he was just returning her car to her home when the police pulled him over. Following the hijacked car at the time of the arrest was a car driven by James Charles, whose name popped up off and on during the trial. Since he never was a witness and with minimum known involvement, I never mentioned him in the story of the trial. Mr. Addison told me that James Charles offered Ms. Rona, the victim of the hijacking, $300-$400 not to testify.

Also rumored on the street was the word that after the robbery-murder James Charles was selling Hennessy on San Bruno Avenue. Despite his efforts, Mr. Addison was unable to get anyone to testify about this.

We know about the threatening phone call from the jail to Mrs. Lee the day before she was murdered. Conjecture is that it was made by Clint Britten. If so, jail rules demand that calls be collect, and there never was any mention of this in the trial.

I asked Mr. Addison what exactly Kris Davis had told him about his whereabouts for that short period of time between his first and second visits to Tucker's house on the early morning of April 3, 1999. Tucker Denton testified that Kris left for a while and then returned, with Tucker seeing him come towards the house from the direction of Harkness Ave., the opposite direction from the KC Market – remember Tucker saying he saw Kris talking to neighbor Mike, who owned a pink VW. Kris told Mr. Addison that he doesn't remember leaving Tucker's after first arriving, and that he more or less remembers just staying in Tucker's bedroom playing video games until Officer Brattan arrived.

Mr. Addison, at our post-trial chat, amplified on what he had mentioned at the close of the trial about the behavior of young men in neighborhoods such as Visitacion Valley when they are questioned by the police. Essentially, they don't tell the truth, even if the truth doesn't hurt them. The jury was exposed to this with the complex, often conflicting testimonies from Tucker Denton, Dominique Lewis, Ricardo Nevins, Harry Norton and Andrew Petty.

Interesting enough, Andrew Petty and Amid Ahmad are the only neighborhood men who do not "own" felony convictions. Today, Mr. Ahmad is one of only five commercial pilots in the U.S. with a Muslim name. He was extremely apprehensive about testifying in this murder trial despite his purely coincidental role. He feared losing his pilot's license.

Kris Davis was accustomed to mistrials. Besides these two on the Lee case, he'd had one in January 1997 when a jury deadlocked eight to four on a case in which a teenage boy was almost murdered in McLaren Park.

Within two minutes after the dismissal of the jury and closure of the trial, Mr. Hallinan told me that "this case will be retried within sixty to ninety days."

APPRECIATION

Wife Diane – Perfect travel and life companion, for her support and advice.

Judith Margolis – A decades-long friend, who repeatedly urged me to write this book.

Son Adam – Who bailed me out of many computer hangups.

Nancy Keller – My editor, with so much know-how and tact in guiding me along the bumpy road.

Mark Weiman – My knowledgeable, patient, and very talented publisher.

Lou Salome – For suggestions and review.

Steve Zolno – Friend for many decades, author and supporter.

ABOUT THE AUTHOR

Jim Breivis, MD retired from the San Francisco Kaiser Permanente Medical Group in 1999. During his tenure he practiced general Orthopedics and served as Chief of the Orthopedics Department, Assistant Chief of Staff of the Medical Center. He was also very involved in local, national and even international medically related organizations and efforts.

None of these stories were pre-planned. All were written as the situations arose and then simply tucked away, until the author's friends urged him to put them into a book.

www.ingramcontent.com/pod-product-compliance
Lightning Source LLC
LaVergne TN
LVHW010418221224
799596LV00002B/4